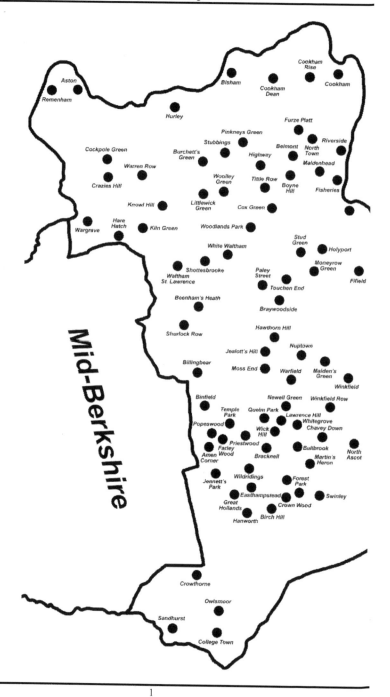

The Towns and Villages of
East Berkshire

EAST BERKSHIRE TOWN and VILLAGE HISTORIES

including Bracknell, Ascot, Windsor, Maidenhead and Slough

Berkshire Town and Village Histories
Volume 1

David Nash Ford

Nash Ford Publishing
Wokingham, Berkshire

Copyright © 2020 David Nash Ford

ISBN 978-1-905191-01-7

First Edition March 2020; Second Edition November 2020
Front cover: Bray, Horton and Easthampstead
Back cover: Town and Village History Coverage

Nash Ford Publishing
Wokingham, Berkshire
www.nashfordpublishing.co.uk
www.berkshirehistory.com

For My Winkfield Girl

Also in this Series

Volume 2: Mid-Berkshire Town and Village Histories
Volume 3: West Berkshire Town and Village Histories

Table of Contents

List of Illustrations

All photographs, maps and illustrations are taken or drawn by David Nash Ford or are antique prints from the Nash Ford Picture Library.

Introduction

Through the latter half of the 20th century and into the new millennium, Eastern Berkshire has become well known for its 'new towns' of Bracknell and Slough and the modern technologies of the companies that have made them their homes. Such growth has changed the landscape and, with it, various parish boundaries and indeed the county boundary itself. Too often now dismissed as a characterless extension of London, the eastern reaches of Berkshire in fact cover a beautiful and diverse region. Each town, village and even suburb has a rich and sometimes surprising history, often shaped by the area's natural features. The River Thames has long been a source of life and work, bringing communications, trade and leisure. However, historically, the major feature of East Berkshire has always been Windsor Forest.

The area around the old Anglo-Saxon palace at Old Windsor was the traditional favourite hunting ground of the Kings of both Wessex and England before the Conquest. Under the Norman kings, this was extended into a formal Royal Forest covering all East Berkshire and parts of Buckinghamshire and Surrey as well. A Royal Forest was not pure woodland but a specified area inhabited by deer and boar, with varied terrain, including open heathland unsuitable for agriculture, administered under forest law. These laws allowed peasants certain rights, but their main purpose was to give the King full control over his pleasure ground without local government interference. Windsor Forest was divided into regions known as bailiwicks, run on the monarch's behalf by the local gentry. Fiennes' Bailiwick, around Binfield, spread across most of the north-west of the Forest. Bataille's Bailiwick, centred on

Sunninghill Park, surrounded Windsor and Ascot. Finchampstead Bailiwick spread across the south, broadly equivalent to the modern Swinley Forest.

Under King James I, the Forest was further subdivided into nine 'walkes,' each centred on a royal hunting lodge. However, the passing of the Windsor Forest Enclosure Act of 1813 effectively put an end to the Forest in this form. Enclosure acts were widely passed for parishes all over the country in order to take shared pasture and agricultural land away from the general populace and to give it to individual landowners. Only a few of the old commons and greens survive today in the area, while landowning estates are manyfold.

Alexander Pope, a local man, best describes this area in his poem, 'Windsor Forest':

Here hills and vales, the woodland and the plain,
Here earth and water, seem to strive again;
Not Chaos like together crush'd and bruis'd,
But as the world, harmoniously confus'd:
Where order in variety we see,
And where, tho' all things differ, all agree.
Here waving groves a checquer'd scene display,
And part admit, and part exclude the day;
As some coy nymph her lover's warm address
Nor quite indulges, nor can quite repress.
There, interspers'd in lawns and opening glades,
Thin trees arise that shun each other's shades.
Here in full light the russet plains extend;
There wrapt in clouds the blueish hills ascend.
Ev'n the wild heath displays her purple dyes,
And 'midst the desart fruitful fields arise,
That crown'd with tufted trees and springing corn,
Like verdant isles the sable waste adorn.

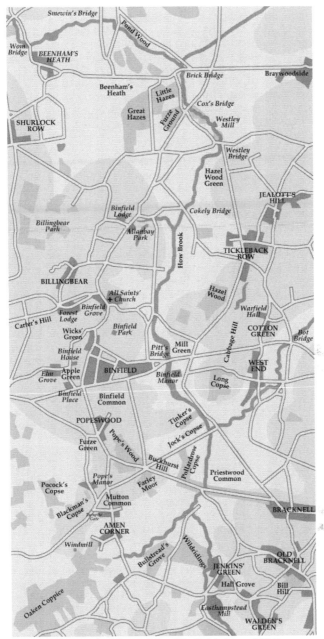

Figure 1: Map of the Binfield Area 1816

Amen Corner, Popeswood and Farley Wood

Amen Corner, in Binfield parish, is at the corner of Beehive Road and North View, down behind the dry ski slope (now closed), where a number of old farms used to cluster. It is supposed to be named after the cries of Baptists returning home from a local chapel, but the name is first recorded in 1846, long before there were non-conformist chapels in this area. As the parish boundary is very close by, it more likely relates to prayers said while 'beating the bounds' of Binfield – an old annual ceremony to confirm the parish boundaries.

This was where the Binfield Brick and Tile Co had their brickworks from 1895 until 1964: one on the site of Octagon House and the car dealership, the other down by the railway, where the old level crossing used to be. However, the name Amen Corner has gradually moved north to refer to the general area around upper Beehive Road and is now even associated with a new estate built on the other side of the London Road.

The Shoulder of Mutton was an early hostelry on this main route out of Bracknell. It was built in the 1820s on 'Mutton Common' where sheep were grazed, but was sadly demolished to make way for an hotel in the late 1990s. It served travellers on the turnpike road (London Road/Wokingham Road rather than the present road of that name) which had opened in about 1770. The turnpike gate stood just to the west, at the junction with Beehive Lane. It was at the adjoining Turnpike Cottage that the turnpike-man, who collected the tolls, was mercilessly shot in 1797. It was suspected that two strangers who had been seen hanging around the local pubs were to blame. The dead man's wife and teenage son had run naked into the road after them but were saved from being shot themselves by the arrival of two gentlemen in a carriage. The 63-year-old turnpike-man was described as "the most inoffensive good-tempered creature living". The area also once had its own windmill, part of which long remained on the site of the Buckhurst Water Treatment Works, near the A329(M) junction.

No matter what modern maps tell you, Popeswood is really the area along the London Road and stretching up the triangle formed by St Mark's Road and Popeswood Road (previously called Deadman's Lane). It was historically called Buckhurst Hill (later corrupted to Bucket Hill) as the rise overlooks Buckhurst (now St Anne's) Manor to the west. However, the area has since been named after the 18th century Pope family. It was probably thought of as an appropriate name for a place adjoining Priestwood. Pope's Manor, in Murrell Hill Lane, has changed names many times, but is now named after this family of a retired Roman Catholic linen-draper, whose son described the place thus:

A little house with trees a-row
And like its master, very low.

The author of these few lines was the famous poet, Alexander Pope, who grew up there from 1700 to 1716. His father constantly encouraged Pope to write verse and it was at this house that he wrote his most famous works, 'Windsor Forest' (1713) and 'The Rape of the Lock' (1714). He drew inspiration from the beautiful countryside around Pope's Meadow (now a public park) where he left the inscription, "Here Pope sung" on one of the old oaks that was sadly chopped down in 1825.

St Mark's Church, at the north end of the triangle, was built between 1865 and 1875. The predecessor of the country house called Moor Close across the road was also built in the former year on the actual site of the wood belonging to the Popes. It was, however, completely remodelled in Arts-and-Crafts style, and the garden laid out by Oliver Hill for the millionaire merchant banker, Charles Birch Crisp, in 1911. Hill was a follower of both Edwin Lutyens and Gertrude Jekyll. The gardens have been fully restored and are occasionally open. The site, along with Popeswood House next door, has since 1945 been part of Newbold College, a higher education college for the Seventh-day Adventists.

Figure 2: Pope's Meadow at Popeswood today with Pope's Tree inset

The Farley Wood estate was built in 1989 on the site of Farley Copse Farm. Some of the road names are quite old and, like Turnpike Road, have been transferred from nearby: Tippett Drive stems from Tippet Lane, an old name for Jock's Lane; Hombrook Drive is a mistake and stems from Howbrook Lane, an old name for the top-end of the Wokingham Road. The stream called The Cut was originally called the How Brook. Just to the north of the estate, down Golden Orb Wood, stands an old house called Farleymoor and, until sadly demolished in recent years, next door was Farley Hall (originally called Farley Copse). The latter was an imposing Victorian Arts-and-Crafts mansion, once the home of Donald JC MacNabb, Deputy Governor of Burma, and then of Mr Arnold Henry Poole. The latter's son, Major John Sanderson Poole, was believed to have died in the First World War, but was only captured by the Germans, escaped three times and eventually made his way back to England. He was captured again in the Second World War but caused so much trouble helping his fellow prisoners to escape that he had to be constantly moved from camp to camp. Farley Moor is the ancient name for the whole area and dates back to at least the early 17th century. The name Golden Orb Wood stems from the Golden Ball Inn which stood at the Popeswood Roundabout, between Jock's Lane and the Wokingham Road, until 1871. It had been there for at least a hundred years and was previously called the Golden Acorn.

Ascot

Ascot was the centre of an important Bronze Age cemetery consisting of a number of round barrows called Bowledge Hill Barrows. Unfortunately, these have almost all been flattened and built upon. Only one survives, bizarrely in the middle of the Heatherwood Hospital complex. An old story tells how they were the home of the mythical Side-hill Winder. This bovine creature had two legs shorter than the others, so it could only live on the side of hills or burial mounds. If you wanted to catch one, you just had to chase it onto level ground where it would fall over.

The name Ascot is Anglo-Saxon and derives from 'East Cote,' the Eastern Cottage, probably a reference to being east of the royal estate at Easthampstead. The place-name and location may have inspired Sir Thomas Malory's Astolat (and Tennyson's Shalott) where, just prior to the Anglo-Saxon period, King Arthur's friend, Sir Lancelot, supposedly stayed with the loyal Sir Bernard. Bernard's daughter, Elaine the Fair, fell in love with the Round Table knight but he did not feel the same. When he left, she died of a broken heart and her body was sent down the Thames in a little boat. It eventually arrived at King Arthur's Court where a letter clutched in her hand explained her story.

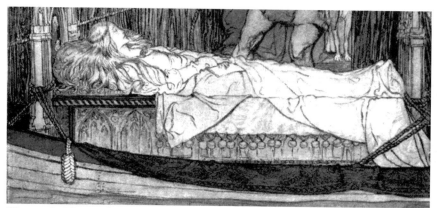

Figure 3: Elaine the Fair drifting down river to King Arthur's Court

Ascot has always been the western portion of Sunninghill parish (now called Sunninghill and Ascot) and, for most of its history, largely consisted of dangerous heathland frequented by highwaymen. John Walsh of Warfield Park is recorded as having shot such a villain of the road whilst crossing Ascot Heath and thought nothing more of it than shooting crows.

Queen Anne liked nothing better than to hunt in Windsor Forest and it was in the early 18th century that she discovered for herself this open heathland which she thought an ideal place, not five miles from Windsor Castle, for "horses to gallop at full stretch". She founded the famous racecourse there in 1711 when the first meet competed for Her Majesty's Plate (worth 100 guineas). The seven runners were sturdy English hunters which had to hold up through three heats, each four miles long. The popularity of Ascot Races died off in later years and, from 1739, an army contingent took to camping on the heath for training purposes and marched to the Battle of Culloden from there seven years later. On their return, they were enlisted in the construction of the Virginia Water.

The races were revived by the Duke of Cumberland in the 1760s. He was Ranger of Windsor Forest, lived at Cumberland Lodge and had his own stud at Cranbourne: hence his interest in racing. His nephew, King George III, was also a great patron and, in the 1790s, set up the first Royal Grandstand (which became known as the Royal Enclosure in 1845). In 1813, this common land was lost to royal hands in the Windsor Forest Enclosure Act. As a result of its popularity, however, the racecourse was made a permanent feature of the landscape for all the public to enjoy.

Early in Queen Victoria's reign, few people lived in Ascot and there was no High Street, just the Ascot Road between Sunninghill and the race course on the Heath. There was a baker's shop and, naturally, a blacksmith near the grandstand. The latter was joined by the, appropriately named, Horse and Groom public house (now Bar 1) next door in 1851. This all began to change in 1856 when the Staines, Wokingham and

Woking Junction Railway reached Ascot, bringing London and its racegoers within easy reach. 1859-61 saw the building of both the Stag pub and Royal Ascot Hotel (on the site of the Grand Regency Heights Apartments). The Heatherwood Roundabout (originally a crossroads), which the latter overlooked, is said to be haunted by the ghost of a policeman of the early motoring age. He was killed there in a horrible accident and his badly scarred face appears illuminated in the headlights of passing cars.

Figure 4: Ascot Races in the 18th century

The gentry also found Ascot attractive and, by the time the station was made an important junction in 1878, a number of small country houses had been built on the southern side of the High Street. Sir Neville Chamberlain, the inventor of snooker (not the Prime Minister) lived at The Wilderness; Arthur Hamilton-Gordon, 1st Baron Stanmore, the colonial governor, lived at the Red House (now Index House); John Delane, the editor of the Times, lived at Ascot Heath House (which replaced an earlier Georgian building); and Charles Lucas of Lucas Brothers, builders of Cliveden House, the Royal Albert Hall and

Alexandra Palace, lived at Heatherwood (previously Heatherfield) which was replaced by the hospital in 1922.

Billingbear

The hamlet of Billingbear is in Binfield parish, but the lost mansion of Billingbear Park was in Waltham St Lawrence. The earliest recorded version of the name is Pullingbere. This could have originally been Phol-Bearo meaning Balder's Sacred Grove. Balder was the son of Woden, the chief of the Anglo-Saxon gods. He was mostly worshipped in Swabia, and a reference in an Anglo-Saxon charter from White Waltham relating to 'Swabian's Hollow' may support this derivation.

Billingbear Park started life as a deer park created for the Bishop of Winchester in 1208. It later became the centre of Binfield Walke (and Fiennes Bailiwick), the greatest of the sixteen red-deer-stocked royal sub-divisions of Windsor Forest. It was granted to Sir Henry Neville, a gentleman of the privy chamber, by King Edward VI in 1551, perhaps as a wedding present. Neville was the younger brother of the 5th Lord Bergavenny and a descendant of the great Neville family of County Durham (as well as Bisham). He had risen to power as a follower of the Duke of Northumberland and even signed the document that left the Crown to the Nine-Days Queen, Lady Jane Grey. He built a magnificent mansion at Billingbear in 1567. It was of the usual Elizabethan red-brick E-shape with multiple gables, which were subsequently removed in the 18th century. Henry's son and namesake was a famous Elizabethan diplomat and there is a bizarre theory that he was the real author of William Shakespeare's plays. During the Civil War, the area was deeply divided: the royalist Colonel Richard Neville of

Billingbear fighting on the opposite side to his parliamentarian brother, Henry. After King Charles II was restored to the Throne, the house was the scene of a great dinner party in 1667. The King, the Duke of York, Prince Rupert and many other nobles rode over from Windsor especially. The Nevilles eventually succeeded to the Braybrooke Barony in 1797. Although the family long retained their second property at Audley End in Essex, sadly their Berkshire house was gutted by fire in 1924, and the remains ruthlessly demolished. It was one of the greatest losses to the county's built landscape.

Figure 5: Billingbear Park in the 17th century

Just north-east of Billingbear hamlet are Allanbay Park and Binfield Lodge. Allanbay (previously called Hall Place, Binfield Place and Diaper's Manor) was first built in the late 18th century, probably by Richard Webb who later inherited Shoppenhangers Manor at Braywick. The Wiggett family – cousins of the Wiggett-Chutes of the Vyne near Basingstoke – owned and extended the place in the Victorian period; but it is most famous for being a hideaway used by Princess Margaret and Group Captain Peter Townsend in the 1950s, when the princess's cousin and lady-in-waiting lived there.

Nearby Binfield Lodge is based around a 16th century hall house reputedly used by James I as a hunting lodge. John Pitt remodelled the place after 1754 for his brother, William (not one of the famous ones), including the addition of pedimented projections copied from his work at Stratfield Saye House. In the 1790s, it was the home of Admiral Sir Edward Vernon (died 1794 and buried in Binfield Church) and then his widow into the 1800s. Vernon had become the hero of the War of Jenkin's Ear against the Spanish when he captured Portobelo in Panama in 1739. He liked to wear coats made of grogram (a silk-wool mix) and thus gave the English language the word 'grog' – which was taken from his nickname of Old Grog – when he ordered sailors' rum to be diluted with water. He also recommended they might add lime (at their own expense) to improve the taste, which may or may not have been the impetus for the eventual order for sailors to eat limes to prevent scurvy. In the 1830s, the Lodge was the home of Edmund Mills, a famous 'wastrel' who was in and out of debtors' prison, and his wife, Emma (formerly Murray). Emma had been the mistress of several men of standing, including Lord Palmerston (the Prime Minister) and the Duke of Buckingham. She had children by both, including the diplomat and writer, Grenville Murray, but they may have spent much of their childhood in London. Ernest Rhodes, brother of the famous colonist of South Africa, Cecil Rhodes, engaged Edwin Lutyens to add a complimentary wing to the house in 1897. The Rhodes family all knew Ernest by the nickname 'Binfield' after the house where he lived.

Binfield

The name Binfield derives from 'Bent Grass Field'. The local hundred (like an ancient district council area) of Beynhurst has a similar derivation. The original village is thought to have been located surrounding and perhaps slightly to the north of the parish church, although it now spreads mostly southwards towards Bracknell. All Saints' Church is a mostly 15th century building with some interesting fittings. Of particular note is the 17th century hourglass and elaborate iron stand, featuring the arms of the Farriers' Company of London, which was used to ensure the rector's sermons were not too long. The famous poet, Alexander Pope, lived at Pope's Manor in Popeswood and sang in the church choir as a boy in the early 1700s; while the artist, John Constable, stayed with friends next door at the rectory (now called the Priory) on his honeymoon in 1816 and twice sketched the church.

Figure 6: Mi'kmaq Native American in Binfield Church

Monuments in the church are dedicated to an array of gentry and nobility who lived in the country houses that sprang up in the district in the 17th and 18th centuries. One is to the historian, Catherine Macaulay Graham (died 1791), who lived at Binfield House, now sheltered accommodation. She was followed there by the Clan Chief and Antiguan sugar planter, William MacKinnon (died 1809), and his family. He was married to the daughter of Admiral Edward Vernon's cousin. This probably explains his attraction to Binfield, as the Admiral lived at Binfield Lodge and also has a monument dedicated to his memory in the church. The heraldic ledger stones to the 4th Countess and 5th Earl of Stirling are quite striking, featuring the native Canadian Mi'kmaq tribesmen of Nova Scotia, a land which had been granted to the 1st Earl by the King. They lived at Lee's House (long demolished) at the bottom of Cabbage Hill, between the Forest Road and Hazelwood Lane.

Just west of the church, on Carter's Hill (previously Orange Hill) stands Billingbear House. It should not be confused with old Billingbear Park and, until 1923, was called Forest Lodge. The house was first built, possibly as early as 1730, by Lieutenant-General Adam Williamson who had served in the War of the Spanish Succession and later became Deputy-Lieutenant of the Tower of London. He was also lord of the manor of Sandhurst but preferred to live in Binfield. He died in 1747 and is buried in Binfield Church. The house was sold by his widow to Commodore Arthur Forrest in 1760. In his early years, he was a protégé of both Admiral Sir Charles Knowles and Admiral Edward Vernon who ended up living in Cranbourne and the Billingbear area of Binfield respectively. He became known for fighting the French in the Caribbean and unexpectedly became default commander-in-chief in Jamaica. As well as a naval officer, Arthur was a rich sugar merchant with six large sugar plantations in Jamaica manned by an abundance of slaves. He used his money to extend his Binfield house with a new suite of rooms, including an octagonal domed music room with Georgian gothic windows and superb Rococo plaster decoration. It was connected to the old house by a picture gallery filled with paintings of the battles in which he had fought. Forrest's wife was buried in Binfield Church and the family continued at the house for another two generations. His grandson, Captain Thomas Forrest, raised eleven children in Jamaica, France and Binfield. Their penultimate child, Haughton, became a noted Australian landscape and marine artist whose work appeared on the first pictorial Australian stamps.

Figure 7: Binfield Manor, built by one of the Pitts in 1754

The village of Binfield that we know today grew up along the Terrace, now Terrace Road North, and Rose Hill. A small hamlet called Emmett's Nest was a later addition, named after George Emmett of Balham who, in the 1820s and 30s, owned the estate that had replaced Lee's House. These three early areas are still remembered in today's road names. Nearby were a number of common greens where the villagers could graze their sheep and cattle. Below what was once Apple (or Apple Pie)

Green is the oldest house in the parish: Binfield Place (formerly Angle's House or Angel House). It is a timber-framed building dating back to Henry VII's reign and was probably built for Robert Sampson, Clerk to the Privy Council. However, it was later encased in brick and converted into a Jacobean E-plan house – although one wing is now missing. The 'Luck of Binfield' was traditionally always housed inside. A 17th century bas-relief of a lady's head, it was said to pour misfortune upon any owner who removed it. To the rear of the grounds was a house named Elm Grove (aka The Grove aka The Elms now rebuilt as Monks' Alley) in the road called Monks' Alley. The original house was said to have been a retreat of the Abbot of Reading: hence the name of the road. However, perhaps the Abbot of Cirencester would be the more likely resident as he owned the right to appoint Binfield's rector. It had its own moat and later appears to have had extensive Elizabethan gardens including a bowling green (covering some kind of ancient earthworks), although it is not known who lived there at the time.

On the east side of the village is the Stag and Hounds, Binfield's most historic inn. Part of it is 14th century. It is said to have been a royal hunting lodge visited by King Henry VIII and Queen Elizabeth I. The latter supposedly used to sit at the window and watch the Maypole dancing on the green outside. Owing to its central position in Windsor Forest, the inn may originally have been the headquarters of the royal gamekeepers. It is, in fact, said to be at the exact centre of the old forest, as marked by the eight-hundred-year-old Centre Elm which once stood immediately outside. The sad hollow trunk of this once great tree – ravaged by Dutch Elm disease in the 1970s – remained for many years until inexplicably removed in 2003.

Forest poachers are said to have cheekily hidden inside it in times gone by, as did a number of parliamentary soldiers during the Civil War. The lodge became a coaching inn in 1727. The 18th century travel writer, William Cobbett, once stayed there and wrote that it was "a very nice country inn," while he called nearby Bracknell a "bleak and desolate" place.

Figure 8: The Stag and Hounds at Binfield

Binfield Park can be glimpsed through the trees on the hillside between the Stag and Hounds and the church. It was built in 1775 for John Elliott, an exceptionally rich factor (a kind of middle man in the cloth trade) from Blackwell Hall, next to the Guildhall, in the City. It eventually passed to his cousin's son, the beautifully named Onesiphorus Elliott Elliott (formerly Ovens). It was later to go to the son of John's maternal 2nd cousin who was the Chaplain to the Duke of Cambridge. However, he got into extreme debt and committed suicide only two years before he would have inherited. His son, George Henry Elliott (formerly Glasse), took the place on, but, perhaps because of his father's earlier troubles, largely rented it out to tenants and lived at the much smaller Hurst Lodge instead. The

Park eventually became a National Health Service residential facility, but in recent years has been turned into apartments.

Further towards Cabbage Hill and Warfield, hidden away opposite what was until recently a garden centre is Binfield Manor, the English home of the Sultan of Brunei. It was built in 1754 for Sir William Pitt of Binfield Lodge (a distant cousin of William Pitt the Elder, Earl of Chatham), at a cost of £36,000. He then moved over from the Lodge and had that rebuilt too. Pitt's Bridge still takes you over the Cut (previously the How Brook) and you can see where it expands to form a lake in the park. Later residents included the banker and art collector, George Kinnaird, 7th Lord Kinnaird, and the Indian administrator, Claude Russell.

For Billingbear Park, see Billingbear

Birch Hill and Hanworth

Birch Hill and Hanworth are two of the housing estates built on the southern edge of Bracknell New Town. The former was built totally within the bounds of South Hill Park. Now an arts centre, the mansion at South Hill was originally put up in 1760 in Italianate style by William Watts, a senior official in the Bengal Army who needed a project on which to spend his Indian gold. He only enjoyed his new home for a further four years until his death in 1764. It later passed through numerous hands, including George Canning who later became Prime Minister, until bought by Sir William Hayter in 1853. Towards the end of the 19th century, his son, Lord Haversham, totally rebuilt the house as the building we see today. South Hill Park has had many well-known visitors over the years: the prime ministers, William Pitt and William Gladstone (who planted a tree in the park) and some say Oscar Wilde, after whom its new theatre is named, although Brook House in Priestwood seems to have been his usual haunt. The building has had rather a sad history over all. Major Rickman, the Haversham heir, being hopelessly in debt, shot himself in the old Gun Room, and there are rumours of other individuals meeting an unfortunate end. It is therefore not surprising that the mansion has an infamous reputation as a haunted house. There are constant unexplained bangs, crashes and doors that become locked of their own accord.

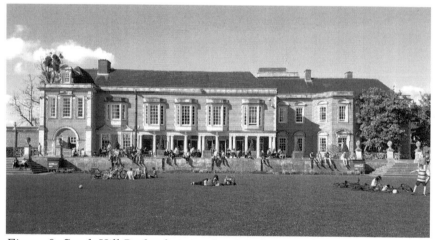

Figure 9: South Hill Park adjoining Birch Hill

The Hanworth housing estate was built in 1971. The name is first mentioned in 1342 but is much older. It is an Anglo-Saxon name meaning High Farm: an individual family settlement on the slopes of Birch Hill. The local pub, though modern, has an interesting name. Whether deliberate or not, the 'Canny Man' can be taken as a reference to the several wizards or cunning men once living at the other end of the county.

Both Birch Hill and Hanworth sit just north of the Nine Mile Ride. The rides were built through Windsor Forest to enable the rotund Queen Anne to follow the hunt in her carriage as she could no longer ride a horse. They were later extended and the Nine Mile Ride laid out by King George III. This ride leads to the site of the old royal kennels at Swinley Lodge near Forest Park. Caesar's Camp is a large Iron Age hillfort lying just south of the Hanworth part of the Nine Mile Ride, near Bracknell's Science Centre, The Look-Out. Coins found there indicate it may date from the first century bc, although it can have little to do with Julius Caesar, who tradition says camped there. It may possibly have been one of the 'oppida' overrun by Vespasian and his Second Legion in AD 47. The name Caesar's Camp only dates from around 1700. The place was originally called Windmill Fort after the mill that stood there.

A group of vicious 18th century bandits known as the Wokingham Blacks because of their camouflaged faces used to meet at the forest lodge adjoining Caesar's Camp. It was there that their leader, William Shorter, was finally captured. The deputy-custodian of Bigshotte Rayles in Crowthorne had been threatened and his house attacked. So, knowing that most of the gang had already been rounded up, he had informed the authorities of a secret rendezvous he was to have with the culprits at the lodge. The Sheriff and his men just had to lie in wait, and Shorter and his gang were sprung like rats in a trap. He was hanged on the county boundary at Wishmoor Cross.

Wickham Bushes, just south of Caesar's Camp, is an area with a Roman-cum-Saxon name meaning Vicus-Home. The prefix is the Latin word for a small Roman town – the successor to the hillfort – some of which was excavated, first in the late nineteenth century and again in more recent years. This indicated it to be a small industrial settlement with numerous wooden and stone houses. In later centuries, military camps were pitched in the area and George III was a frequent visitor to review the troops.

Bisham

Marlow Bridge is, of course, half in Bisham. There has been a bridge there (or just slightly to the east) since at least 1309, originally under the patronage of the Knights Templar, a monastic order of soldiers created to protect pilgrims heading for the Holy Land. During the Civil War of the 17th century, the roundhead army slighted the old bridge and made it impassable for a while, but it was quickly repaired. In 1789, a new version was built, and raised up to allow for the increased height of boats passing beneath. The present suspension bridge, designed by William Tierney Clark, was built in 1829-32. It has a similar big brother, by the same architect, crossing the Danube in the centre of Budapest called the Széchenyi Chain Bridge.

The riverside part of Bisham parish consists of the village of Bisham and the hamlet of Temple. Temple seems to have started out as an Iron Age farmstead with a roundhouse and associated complex of grain storage pits, some of them dedicated to the gods with dead animal parts. The site continued in use into Roman times when a rectangular wooden house with a chalk floor was built. The owners farmed mostly cattle. In the Middle Ages, the area became the site of Temple Mills built on the Mill Island (now a housing estate with its own marina), which had belonged to the Knights Templar resident at Bisham Manor. In the early 18th century, copper and brass pans and utensils, as well as sheet copper, were produced there, as referred to by Daniel Defoe in his 'Tour thro' the Whole Island of Great Britain' (1727). By the end of the century, the hammer mill, flat rolling mill and bolt mill there were part of the vast empire of the 'Copper King,' Thomas Williams. Much of his copper is said to have been traded in Africa for slaves going to the West Indies, but he also provided the copper cladding and bolts for Nelson's ships during the Napoleonic Wars. Williams had the magnificent classical Temple House built just to the west of the mills, in 1790. This was the Williams' English family home for several generations of Marlow MPs, including Thomas' grandson, the Father of the House of Commons, Lieutenant-Colonel Thomas Peers Williams. Unfortunately, the house burnt down in 1910.

Figure 10: Bisham 'Abbey,' the Preceptory Hall of the Knights Templar

Bisham village itself was an Anglo-Saxon settlement named after Baessel's Water Meadow. It was early chosen as the site of a preceptory (like a monastery) for the Knights Templar who were given the manor in the 1140s. At the centre of the complex was what is currently called the 'abbey' – actually a fine example of a medieval manor house with later additions. The main feasting hall was built for these crusading knights-cum-monks in about 1260, along with a separate circular chapel, the remains of which are apparently now buried under the tennis courts. The order was suppressed in 1307, when the Crown took the place over and used it as a luxurious prison for King Robert the Bruce's queen and daughter, captured during the Scottish Wars of Succession.

Figure 11: Bisham Priory from the Earldom of Salisbury Roll circa 1463

Eventually, in 1335, the manor came into the hands of William, 3rd Baron Montacute. He was a close friend of King Edward III and was sent to arrest the Earl of March who had had Edward's father murdered. He extended the end of the Templar hall with living quarters and a small cloistral arcade that can still be seen today. In 1337, Montacute was rewarded with the Earldom of Salisbury and, in the same year, he founded a priory for Austin canons immediately adjacent to, and completely dominating, his manor house at Bisham. It was only briefly raised to the status of an abbey just before its dissolution, but this is the name that has survived, but transferred to the manor house. Bisham was an ideal location for a large-scale building project like this, as many villagers were then employed in quarrying and supplied much of the stone for Windsor Castle. The name of Quarry Woods still reminds us of the quarry's location. The eerie wood was later the inspiration for Kenneth Grahame's 'Wild Wood' where Mr Badger lived in his novel, the 'Wind in the Willows'. Some people also think that Quarry Wood Hall, on the Thames, inspired Toad Hall. Grahame wrote his famous book at nearby Cookham Dean.

The foundation stone of Bisham Priory was laid by King Edward III himself and the brass plaque recording the event can now be seen reused in Denchworth Church, near Wantage. The Priory held minor relics of Saints Cosmas and Damian, but never became a major pilgrimage centre and, despite the resident patronage of the Salisburys, remained a relatively poor monastery. However, it was soon to become the family mausoleum and the medieval monuments there must have rivalled those at places like Tewkesbury Abbey in Gloucestershire:

- William Montacute, 1st Earl of Salisbury, who was killed in a joust in 1344, and his wife.
- William, died 1383, son of William Montacute, 2nd Earl of Salisbury

- William Montacute, 2nd Earl of Salisbury, who died in 1397 leaving instructions for suitable monuments to be erected to himself, his son and his parents.
- John Montacute, 3rd Earl of Salisbury, who was beheaded by a mob for attempting to restore King Richard II to his throne during the 'Epiphany Rising' in 1400, and his wife.
- Thomas Montacute, 4th Earl of Salisbury, the most skilful English soldier to fight in the Hundred Years' War with France, and his two wives. He was killed at the Siege of Orleans in 1428 when a cannon ball struck him in the face while he stood at an open window. A depiction of him, with the three-tiered monument described in his will, may be seen in the east window of Bisham Church.
- Richard Neville, 5th Earl of Salisbury, a leading Yorkist in the Wars of the Roses who was killed after the Battle of Wakefield in 1460, and his wife, Alice, daughter of the 4th Earl. His head was stuck on a spike on Micklegate Bar in York but the rest of his body was eventually brought to Bisham. His effigial monument has survived and, for reasons unknown, can be seen in Burghfield Church, near Reading.
- Sir Thomas, son of Richard Neville, 5th Earl of Salisbury, who was also killed at Wakefield in 1460. He was also decapitated.
- John Neville, Marquess of Montague, son of Richard Neville, 5th Earl of Salisbury, who was killed at the Battle of Barnet in 1471.
- Richard Neville 'Warwick the Kingmaker,' 6th Earl of Salisbury and 16th Earl of Warwick. This was the man whose support determined whether King Henry VI or King Edward IV sat on the Throne. He was killed at the Battle of Barnet in 1471.
- Prince Edward, 8th Earl of Salisbury and 18th Earl of Warwick, son of Prince George, Duke of Clarence. He was executed in 1499 because he was a rival for King Henry VII's throne.
- Arthur Pole, son of Sir Richard Pole and Princess Margaret, Countess of Salisbury, who died 1528.

In the early 15th century, the manor passed to the great northern family of Neville, whose central role in the Wars of the Roses cannot be overestimated, in particular the actions of King Edward IV's cousin, the all-powerful Earl of Warwick 'the

Kingmaker'. Although they spent much time on their Yorkshire estates and in London, their Southern country residence was Bisham Manor. The Bull Inn at Bisham was named after their family symbol. Built for the village mason who put up the church, it is said to have been a pub for about six hundred and fifty years, with reputed visits from Templars, Henry VIII and Elizabeth I. Within, there is a superb stained-glass window showing the head of a large black bull surrounded by crests of the lords of the manor.

Figure 12: Sir William Montacute arrests Roger Mortimer, Earl of March

After the Wars, Princess Margaret, Countess of Salisbury – the niece of Edward IV and Richard III – eventually managed to regain her house at Bisham and built the marvellous dovecote, still to be seen today, in order to provide sustenance for her household through the winter. She was governess to Princess Mary (later Queen Mary Tudor) and they spent some time there together. Being a good Catholic, the Countess rebuked the commissioners who closed and then demolished the Priory in 1536. She is said to have tried to save the family monuments by gathering them together in the old feasting hall.

After the Countess's execution, resulting from her claim to the Throne, Bisham came into the hands of Sir Philip Hoby and his brother, Sir Thomas. They were both English ambassadors in Europe and erected the rest of the house, including the tower. Sir Philip was amongst the many courtiers of King Henry VIII who were painted by Hans Holbein the Younger. Through Sir Thomas' wife, Lady Elizabeth, the brothers later had connections with some of the most influential people at the Elizabethan Court, including her brother-in-law, Lord Burghley, the Queen's chief advisor. As Princess Elizabeth, the Queen had been kept in their care at Bisham for several years. She apparently used to drink from the holy well named after her and planted a mulberry tree still standing in the grounds. Elizabeth, Lady Hoby is said to have been a singularly stern individual. Being highly educated, she took to tutoring her own children. One son, however, was such a disappointment to her that she could not help but lose her temper with him. One day she is said to have beaten him to death with a ruler for having accidentally made ink blots all over his exercise book. Her repentant ghost is often seen around the Abbey, ceaselessly washing her blood-stained hands.

Lady Elizabeth's monument, in the southern Hoby Chapel of Bisham Church, is one of the largest and most spectacular of any to be found outside a cathedral. It features the lady and all her children. The youngest, Sir Thomas Posthumous Hoby, is claimed to have been the inspiration for Malvolio in William

Shakespeare's 'Twelfth Night'. Lady Hoby organised both this monument and her own funeral down to the last detail, even writing to the College of Arms to confirm her heraldic rights and privileges. Her husband and brother-in-law recline alongside her with hobby hawks at their feet. It is a very early monument of its type, probably made in France. However, it is the swan-covered obelisk to her daughter-in-law, Margaret Carey Hoby, which commands one's attention. This lady was the daughter of Queen Elizabeth I's cousin, Lord Hunsdon, and she was visited at the 'Abbey' by her royal relative. The early 17th century heraldic windows trace the Hoby family history.

Figure 13: The Hoby Monuments in Bisham Church

In 1780, a younger branch of the Vansittart family from Shottesbrooke Park purchased the Bisham estate. They later became the Vansittart-Neales. They are particularly remembered by a sad monument in the church to their heir, an

Eton boy who died of appendicitis at the age of only fourteen in 1904. He is represented along with his spaniel, Norman, sculpted from life. He was one of several young Vansittarts and their heirs who died in tragic circumstances, giving rise to talk of a curse on the owners of the house. After the Second World War, Bisham Abbey house was lent, and later sold, to the Central Council for Physical Recreation as a sports training centre in memory of the two heirs killed in the War. The family then moved into the adjoining Bisham Grange. The Abbey house and its grounds are now one of the country's National Sports Centres.

The Grange was the 16th century home farm, later used as a bailiff's and then a dower house, and largely rebuilt in Victorian times. The Bisham estate, including the pub, the shop and all the houses in the village, was run like one big family, with the Vansittart-Neales knowing all their tenants by name and looking after their needs. However, in 1965, the last of the family, Mrs Elizabeth Paget, died and the estate was inherited by her cousin's daughter, Miss Margaret Dickinson. With death duties running at 65%, she was forced to sell the entire village for just £30,000. This was to change village life there forever.

Boyne Hill, Altwood and Tittle Row

There appears to have been a Roman settlement at Altwood. A ditched enclosure with a tile kiln has been discovered where the road called Altwood Bailey now stands. Domestic pottery and animal bones from the site were dated to AD 150. 'Alt' is Celtic for a small wood, a name which the incoming Anglo-Saxons evidently did not understand, so they added their own 'wood' on the end. Altwood and Tittle Row are basically the same place. Tittle Row is the newer name and may not be particularly ancient. Originally Tittle Back Row, it referred to a row of houses along the north side of Altwood Road, in the area immediately east of the A404(M). They adjoined Altwood House which stood where Holmwood Close is now. In the 19th century, it was the home of a local landlord, Joseph Henry Clark, and later a retired army captain, George Lloyd Robson.

Figure 14: All Saints' Church, Boyne Hill with its detached tower

Boyne Hill – possibly Bofa's Hill – started out as a small hamlet in Ive's manor in Bray parish. It was originally centred on the crossroads of Altwood Road, Boyne Valley Road and Norden Road, by the Crown pub. In the early 19th century, it began to spread up Westborough Road where two more popular pubs, the Pond House and the Crooked Billet, were built. The old pond after which the pub is named is now covered by its car park.

A few doors north of the Crooked Billet stood a house that became notorious for a horrible murder that occurred there in 1852. It was the home of a farm labourer, John Cannon, his wife Elizabeth and five of their children, including the eldest, James, who was married with a little girl of his own: Lizzie, aged four. Also living with them was Elizabeth's brother, Isaac Lee, a successful Bermondsey brush-maker, who had had mental health issues since the death of his wife. He had ended up in the Bethlehem Hospital – commonly called Bedlam – but had persuaded his sister to let him move into her Boyne Hill home in return for a substantial financial incentive. Despite a long period of sanity, Isaac remained susceptible to bouts of extreme anger. One March morning, when Elizabeth popped out to see a neighbour, he saw red when a young piglet ran into the house looking for scraps. Isaac viciously attacked the creature with a billhook before turning on little screaming Lizzie when she tried to escape the gory scene.

Figure 15: William Gresley's Memorial Brass at Boyne Hill

Not long afterwards, however, Boyne Hill became a popular suburb of Maidenhead when the striking church of All Saints' was built in Boyne Hill Road in 1855-7. It is a triumphant piece of decorative brickwork by GE Street, a pupil of George Gilbert Scott, follower of Augustus Pugin and a great champion of the Victorian Gothic revival style. All Saints' was his very first ecclesiastical commission, but he is best known for having designed the Royal Courts of Justice on the Strand. Shortly before building work commenced at Boyne Hill, Street had married Mariovita Procter from Bray and she was buried in the churchyard upon her death in 1874. The church was planned as just part of a larger complex around a quadrangle, including vicarage, coach house, stables, schoolroom and master's house, by the Misses Emily and Maria Hulme, daughters of the Rector of Shinfield, near Reading. There was also a house for their retirement. The prominent, and originally detached, tower and spire of the church was not added until 1864. Congregations were visited by Prime Minister William Gladstone and the Italian general, Giuseppe Garibaldi, and grew so huge that the nave had to be extended in 1911 by Street's son.

The first vicar, William Gresley has an effigial brass memorial (1876) on the floor of the chancel: a superb example of Victorian Gothic revival art. Adjoining it is a less elaborate version to his successor Canon Arthur Hislop Drummond (1925). His son, Malcolm Drummond, was born and brought up at the Vicarage and went on to become a prominent member of the Camden Town Group and then the London Group of post-impressionist artists. He was noted for his paintings of domestic interiors and urban landscapes. His works include several of Boyne Hill Church, Vicarage and the vicarage garden.

After the First World War, a house called Recess at Boyne Hill became the home of the classical archaeologist, Ernest Gardner, during his retirement. He had excavated in Egypt, Cyprus and Greece but spent most of his career as the Director of the British School at Athens and in various high-level posts at the University of London, including Yates Professor of Classical Art and Archaeology and Public Orator. He was also editor of the Journal of Hellenistic Studies. His daughter, Phyllis Gardner, was a well-known Irish wolf-hound breeder and artist. She founded the Coolafin Kennels at their home. She was also a suffragette and had earlier been the lover of poet, Rupert Brooke.

Bracknell

The name Bracknell derives from Braccen-Heale meaning Bracken covered Nook. It is mentioned in a Winkfield Boundary Charter of AD 942. The original Anglo-Saxon settlement was probably at Old Bracknell, which spreads out along Old Bracknell Lane. By 1607, there was already a substantial 'New' Bracknell (at the time often called Bracknell Street) along the current High Street. It had developed as a stopping point on the route from London to Reading via Staines. Traditionally, this started out, in the 16th century, with just the Old Manor, now a pub and restaurant, and the long lamented Hind's Head pub on the very edge of the lawless Sker and Whit Moors and the heathland beyond that could not be crossed safely at night. However, this ribbon settlement dates back to at least 1400, the time when the Bull Inn and the old building in Union Square now housing an estate agency were built as medieval hall-houses. Further down the High Street, another surviving hostelry, the Red Lion (now a smokehouse restaurant), dates from only a hundred years later.

By the 17th century, Bracknell had become the location for three annual fairs, held in April, August and October. This made the place a popular trading centre, though the cruel entertainments of bull baiting and cock fighting were also popular. In the 19th century, an important cattle market was opened behind the Hind's Head (beneath Bracknell and Wokingham College).

Figure 16: The old Hind's Head and Royal Forest Hotel, Bracknell

The now demolished Hind's Head Pub had a particularly unsavoury reputation. In the 18th century, its publican apparently came up with an ingenious way of subsidising his income. Any rich traveller who stopped at the inn was given a particularly undesirable room for the night: It had a trap door beneath the bed. When asleep, the unfortunate guest would be tipped down a neck-braking shaft and their possessions taken to swell the innkeeper's purse. Eventually, a barmaid fell for one of the prospective murder victims and told him what to expect. He ran for help and the publican was quickly arrested. Unfortunately for Bracknell, this story is almost identical to the much better documented version from the Ostrich Inn in Colnbrook.

The current Old Manor pub, an early 16th century country house, is just across the road from the site of the Hind's Head (to the west). It has a beautiful brick frontage added a hundred years later. The building is famous locally for its priest hole, overlooking one of the bars, used to hide Catholic priests during the persecuting Tudor period. It is said to have secret passages connecting to various locations, including the old Hind's Head. Legend associates them with Dick Turpin, an unlikely patron. Use of the underground passages by the secret priests would seem more likely. However, the story does demonstrate the surrounding area's infamy as the haunt of bandits. A few doors down on the site of the old Post Office (now a restaurant), stood the Round House or town lock-up, where such miscreants were held before being transferred to Wokingham. It wasn't too uncomfortable, as friends were able to pass pints through the grill in the door from the adjoining Crown Inn, built in 1644 (but demolished in 1930).

It was at Bracknell, in 1723, that a troop of mounted grenadier guards fought a pitched battle with the infamous band of local criminals known as the Wokingham Blacks (because of their muddied faces). They had been marauding around this area of Windsor Forest for over a year, but, after one of their number was forced to reveal the gang's whereabouts, the authorities were, at last, able to capture some twenty-nine men.

The main road through the town became a Turnpike in 1759, with a gate and a cottage to collect tolls at Lily Hill in Bullbrook. The town had had a forge since at least 1680 and the local Post Office was established there in the early 19th century. All this increased the number of coaches – including the Wokingham Flying Machine and the Reading Flying Machine – bringing more genteel visitors. A one-time resident of the town was the celebrated poet, Percy Bysshe Shelley. During the period of his rocky first marriage, in 1813, he took a fancy to a certain Mrs Cornelia Turner and moved to a house called High Elms in Bracknell to be with her. This house stood at the junction of Park Road and Warfield Road, in what is now the middle of the Met Office Roundabout. They studied the Italian poets together, but how far their relationship went otherwise is unclear.

Figure 17: Lawrence's Stores in Bracknell High Street

Congregational ministers had been preaching in Bracknell in the late 18th century and, by 1822, they had their own church in the High Street (since demolished). The Church of England Church of Holy Trinity was not built until 1851 and, five years later,

Bracknell gained its own railway station. The town became a thriving Victorian community with a busy High Street. This was particularly enhanced by Thomas Lawrence's Bracknell Supply Stores. Jam-packed with products of all descriptions, this astonishing department store was built in 1885, in neo-Elizabethan style, to show off the TLB bricks produced at Lawrence's own Warfield Brickworks at Lawrence Hill. Another fine building was the clock-tower bedecked Royal Forest Hotel, opposite the Manor. The clock itself actually survives, incorporated into the modern building on the site.

Figure 18: The Crossway, Bracknell (since demolished)

Lawrence had a number of brickworks that employed hundreds of local people. In the Arlington Square area, between Skimped Hill Lane and Easthampstead Road, stood his Easthampstead Brickworks between 1892 and 1908. Across Easthampstead Road, on the Western Industrial Estate, the Bracknell Business Centre in Downmill Road stands on the site of another brickworks, that of the Down Mill (Bracknell) Brick Co which operated from 1903 and was taken over by the Maidenhead Brick and Tile Co from Pinkneys Green in 1920. The brickfield spread to the east.

In 1949, Bracknell was chosen as the site of a 'New Town' for 25,000 people from bombed-out London after White Waltham had been rejected as unsuitable. The first new residents moved in in 1951 but, ten years later, an increase of homes for another 35,000 residents was planned, including the total rebuild of the town centre in 1966 with the loss of almost all the old buildings in the High Street. Major new employers moved to the town, particularly electronics companies, including Racal in 1954, Ferranti in 1956, Sperry Gyroscope in 1957 and the Met Office in 1961. Sadly, all these are now gone, although Sperry's is remembered by the Gyroscope sculpture on the roundabout still named after the company. Currently, the town's largest employer is Waitrose, which moved their headquarters there in 1972. New housing estates have, of course, continued to be added up to the present day.

Bray

No-one seems to be able to agree on the meaning of the name Bray. The Thames in this area seems to have been honoured by Iron Age warriors as a holy place into which to throw treasured weapons as a sacrifice to the river spirits. One such object, the 33-inch-long Amerden Sword and scabbard, with typical interlaced circle and triskele decoration, can been seen in the British Museum. Bray was once thought to have been Bibrax (or Bibracte) to the Romans, but this place never existed and was made up by the medieval cartographic forger, Richard of Cirencester. There does appear to have been Roman activity in the parish, however, especially in the Water Oakley area.

The old Anglo-Saxon church was also said to have been at Water Oakley. It was pulled down in 1293 ready for rebuilding in the main village in Early English style, as approved by all the parishioners. However, when the churchwardens came to collect everyone's contribution to the construction work, some would not pay and they had to send out the beadle to enforce the agreement. An old legend tells how there was initially trouble with demons pulling down the new building work.

A supposed broken 'Sheela-Na-Gig,' up in the rafters of the present church, may have come from the old building. This Irish name refers to a small stone female figure with large breasts and legs spread wide representing the Celtic mother goddess and incorporated into churches to remind the faithful of the temptations of the old religion. A less controversial relic of the old Anglo-Saxon church is the carving of a horse or a dog encased in the walls of the Chantry Chapel of Our Lady that stands in the churchyard. It had its own chantry priest who lived in the cottage built over the lychgate in 1448. This later became the Six Bells Inn, named after the instruments hanging in the church. The parish church has two further chantry chapels within its walls, built to pray for the souls of the founders: the Foxley Chapel of All Saints at the end of the south aisle and the Norreys Chapel of St Nicholas in the north aisle. The building has some fine monuments, some moved from these chapels and others long lost. The superb brass to the armoured Sir John Foxley (died 1378), from Foxley Manor at Touchen End, and his two wives in their heraldic dresses commemorates a soldier of the Hundred Years' War. He and his first wife eloped together at the age of only fourteen. The monuments to two branches of the Norreys family from Fifield and Ockwells at Cox Green have largely disappeared. Sir John, the builder of Ockwells House and the Lancastrian Master of the Royal Wardrobe during the Wars of the Roses, left instructions for his burial at Bray in an impressive marble tomb in 1467. Only his beaver-supported coat-of-arms survives on the wall, but there is also a 1591 incised mural slab to William Norreys of Fifield, the 'Black Rod' to Queen Elizabeth I. Perhaps the finest monument features the striking demi-figure sculptures of William Goddard and his wife, who founded the Jesus Hospital in 1609. This beautiful almshouse, with his full-height statue over the entrance, was built to house thirty-four of the parish's aged poor, as well as six from the Fishmongers' Company to which Goddard belonged and is still in use on the road to Holyport.

Figure 19: Sir John Foxley's Brass in Bray Church

The Hind's Head in the village is a 15th century hall-house. Its origins are obscure, but it may have been a royal hunting lodge or cottages for the church builders. It was certainly a guesthouse of the Abbot of Cirencester who owned Bray Church from

1133. The Duke of Edinburgh held his stag party there in 1947. It is now a single Michelin starred gastro pub owned by Heston Blumenthal, who also owns the Crown. Bray is most famous as the location of the only restaurants outside London with 3-Michelin stars, both Alain Roux's Waterside Inn and Blumenthal's Fat Duck. In centuries past, however, it was best known as the home of the 'Singing Vicar of Bray,' the star of a well-known ballad. He supposedly promised to remain "the Vicar of Bray, Sir" no matter what religious denomination he had to adopt. The ballad indicates he was Francis Carswell (Vicar 1650-1709), but the story was recorded of the rector, as early as 1662, through the turbulent Tudor years. This period has two possible candidates: Simon Simonds (1523-47), an ancestral cousin of the Reading brewers and brother of one of the Windsor Martyrs, whose death could have inspired his maxim; or Simon Alleyn (Vicar 1523-65) who was buried in the middle of the nave after a very long service as vicar.

A famous hotel not far east of the village is the Monkey Island Hotel, named after the islet in the Thames on which it stands. The name is popularly supposed to recall the painted monkeys fishing and shooting on the hotel ceiling. However, it was originally Monk's Eyot and was used by the brethren from Merton Priory's grange at Taplow. For centuries the island was part of the Whiteknights Estate in Earley and, in 1744, the 3rd Duke of Marlborough had a fishing lodge and banqueting temple built there for use when attending the Kit-Kat Gentlemen's Club at Down Place in Water Oakley: hence the fishing monkeys painted by Andrieu de Clermont. However, a romantic old story, with no evidence, suggests they actually represent the pet monkey of King George III who was allowed to stay there during his fits of madness. In 1840, the two buildings were expanded and converted into a hotel which has always been popular with high society. HG Wells and his lover, Rebecca West, were frequent visitors and the latter set her first book, 'Return of the Soldier,' there. King Edward VII and Queen Alexandra were also particularly fond of the place.

Figure 20: The Jesus Hospital of 1609 at Bray

Braywick

Braywick is one of the earliest places settled in the Thames Valley. Excavations have shown that Mesolithic man undertook flintworking there producing finely worked microliths. Neolithic man followed and it is believed that his pottery found in the area is some of the earliest ever discovered in Britain, from around 3,340 bc.

The present village appears to date from the arrival of the Anglo-Saxons in the 5th century. The sunken workshops of a farmstead have been excavated on the site of the leisure centre and occupation there lasted for about 200 years. The word 'wick' most commonly indicates an Anglo-Saxon settlement based around a dairy farm. This one was originally associated with the manor of Shoppenhangers, which means Hanging Woods i.e. hillside woods on Harvest Hill. Throughout the 17th and 18th century it was one of the main homes of the Winch family who were widespread in Bray parish. The most recent manor house was scandalously demolished in 2007, despite being very attractive and quite unique. It gave the appearance of being 17th century but was built in 1915 by an antique dealer from Sussex. He used completely authentic salvaged materials throughout the building, including some from the old manor house of Foxleys at Touchen End.

Figure 21: Shoppenhangers Manor, built in 1915 and demolished in 2007

Bray Wick was one of the ancient tithings of the parish of Bray. Local records in 1517 show that the 'tithingman' in charge there was somewhat intolerant and threatened an unfortunate lady named Alice Smythgate with a fine and "bodily punishment" if she did not refrain from "babbling" and using her "unruly tongue". In the next century, the village was known for its windmill which stood on Windmill Hill.

Another manor in Braywick, on Canon Hill, was owned by Reinbald the Priest, Dean of the Prebendary College at Cirencester at the time of the Domesday Book (1086). He was rector of some 30 churches across the country, Bray amongst them. In the late 13th century, the manor passed to Cirencester Abbey and the Abbot appears to have had an extensive grange (or farming) complex there. Canon Hill House was a 17th century mansion built on the site with later Adams' ceilings and a private chapel. It was demolished in 1973. Well-House, built on the Kitchen Garden of Canon Hill House was so named because it had a well used as an ice-house. The ice used to be brought by horse and cart from Slough. The beams in the house were said to be made from ship-timbers.

Braywick House (previously Braywick Grove) was built for Sir William Paule, the Bishop of Oxford's son, in 1675. It is now offices but can be easily viewed from the main Maidenhead Road. There are stories of smugglers' tunnels for bringing wine up from the Thames and, at an earlier building, Oliver Cromwell is said to have imprisoned royalist captives while stabling parliamentary horses in the cellars during the Civil War. The 18th century Braywick Lodge, home of the Hibbert family, no longer stands, but its grounds are a public park and Hibbert Road remembers their name. The mid-Victorian villa, Stafferton Lodge (previously spelt Staverton Lodge), is now a popular restaurant. It was built on the site of a secondary home of the Tudor Staverton family of Stroud Manor at Holyport. The original building at Braywick was called 'Little Stroud'.

Britwell and Manor Park

Haymill is the area around Burnham Station in Slough. As Burnham Beeches Station, this was opened in 1899. Burnham proper is over the border in Buckinghamshire. Hay Mill (aka Ay Mill) on the Two-Mile Brook stood where the flats at Priory Heights are now. To the north, the Haymill Valley Nature Reserve marks the site of the old millpond. The site had a mill before 1268. It was part of the liberty of Cippenham and was given to Burnham Abbey by Prince Richard, Earl of Cornwall. Just before the Dissolution of the Monasteries, their tenants used it as a brewery. Later, it was sub-let, but the main tenant retained the right to breed swans on the mill pond.

Figure 22: Baylis House, built in 1696 for the Dean of Windsor

Baylis House (aka Whitmarsh Manor) stands in Stoke Poges Lane, at the southern end of Manor Park, an area that was historically the southern portion of Stoke Poges parish. In the late 19th century, it was sometimes referred to as Stoke-in-Slough. The manor seems to have been established in the late 15th century. The present house is a beautiful Dutch style mansion, built in 1696 for the Dean of Windsor, Reverend Doctor Gregory Hascard. The architect is traditionally said to have been Sir Christopher Wren, but a young John James of Greenwich, who certainly later made alterations there, may be more likely. After Hascard's death, another cleric, Reverend Doctor Henry Godolphin, Dean of St Paul's and Provost of Eton, moved in: hence the nearby Godolphin Playing Fields. In the 18th century, his descendants, the Osborne family, rented it out to a number of interesting tenants: The statesman and diplomat, Philip Dormer Stanhope, 4th Earl of Chesterfield, commissioned the first Chesterfield sofa but is also well known for his published letters to his illegitimate son, many of which were written at Baylis; Charles II's grandson, William FitzRoy, 3rd Duke of Cleveland; and the Attorney General and Lord Chancellor, Alexander Wedderburn, 1st Earl of Rosslyn, who was visited at Baylis by King George III despite Society considering him "not only dull himself, but [to have] inspired dullness in others". Later a Roman Catholic School, the house was saved from demolition by its purchase, in 1939, by the local council and is currently an hotel.

Not far away, also in Stoke Poges Lane, stands the old Horlicks Factory, a fine example of early 20th century industrial architecture. James Horlick, a chemist from Gloucestershire, developed his malted milk drink in London, but first manufactured it with his brother in America before returning to England and building his factory in Slough in 1908. He was made a baronet in 1914 and by 1969, the factory was producing 30 million pounds of powdered drink a year. The factory was closed by GlaxoSmithKline in June 2018 and all but the clock tower and chimney are due for residential redevelopment.

Most of industrial Slough, however, developed after the First World War. An area around the railway, near Cippenham, was purchased by the Government in late 1918 for the building of a large motor repair depot to supply the army then fighting in Europe. However, the War came to an end shortly afterwards and the wooden buildings erected for the soldiers were turned into housing for the unemployed of the following decades. It was known locally as Timbertown. In 1920, Sir Percival (later Lord) Perry, the Chairman of Ford Motors in the UK, led a consortium which bought the 600-acre site, including 17,000 used vehicles for refurbishment and 4 acres of workshops. These latter were eventually leased out to local businesses and Slough Trading Estate was born. By the 1930s, it had a workforce of 23,000 people who were soon provided with their own banks, post office, community centre, health service and power station. Today the company boasts that it is the largest industrial estate in single private ownership in Europe.

By the late 1930s, the Manor Park housing estate for the workers had begun to be developed along the Farnham Road on agricultural land previously called Stoke Great Field. During the Second World War, much of the trading estate was turned over to war work, including the manufacturing of Spitfire parts and incendiary bombs. Amongst the smaller businesses that have operated there since, perhaps the most well known is AP Films where, in the 1960s, Gerry and Sylvia Anderson produced the children's television classics, Stingray (1964-65), Thunderbirds (1965), Captain Scarlet (1967) and others. Amongst the larger well-known companies on the estate, the Mars factory was founded, as a very small establishment, by the American, Forrest Mars Senior, in 1932. The first Mars Bars in the World were made in Slough in that year and were joined by Maltesers four years later and many other chocolate greats since. The present factory produces 3 million Mars Bars a day.

Figure 23: The Horlicks Factory (1908) on the edge of Manor Park

Britwell was historically in the middle of the eastern portion of the Buckinghamshire parish of Burnham. It was originally a small hamlet consisting of Britwell House (now an accountancy firm at Grenville Court) and a number of surrounding farms in an area still over the county boundary today. The bright well after which it was named is supposed to have been in Green Lane.

Britwell in Slough was built on the farmland of Biddles Farm on Lynch Hill. This was purchased by London County Council after the Second World War to build new homes for those from bombed-out Paddington, West Kensington and Shepherd's Bush. 11,000 tenants began to move in in 1956, but there were no local facilities or easy access to Slough town centre until after 1959 when the Community Association successfully campaigned for a community centre and local bus service. The area was home to sometime Home Secretary (2009-10), Alan

Johnson MP, who first became an active trade unionist while working as a local postman. Britwell became a civil parish and was transferred into Berkshire in 1974. However, the social housing there remained under the control of the Greater London Council until 1986.

Bullbrook and Whitegrove

In the mid-18th century, Bulbrook consisted of a handful of houses on the edge of Chavey Down. However, a toll house for the new turnpike road was built in this area in 1759, after which the place grew into a small village, centred around Bulbrook Farm and Bridge, at the junction of Jig's Lane with the London Road. The Royal Oak is one of the older remaining buildings and seems to date back to the 1830s. The Running Horse is, of course, a modern pub but there was previously an earlier building on the other side of the London Road. The modern housing estate of Bullbrook was built in the late 1950s after Bracknell was chosen to become a 'New Town' for the people of war-torn London. It was supposed to have completed the original planned town but plans change and Bracknell has expanded much since. The area is named after the Bull Brook which emerges above ground near the eastern end of Holly Spring Lane.

On the edge of Bullbrook stands Lily Hill Park. This lovely old house was built in 1817 by Henry Dormer Vincent, possibly on the site of a medieval hunting lodge. Henry was an equerry to HRH The Duke of Gloucester and probably moved to Bullbrook to be near him at Bagshot Park. The Vincent family and their heirs, the Lanes, lived at Lily Hill for almost a hundred years, making extensive alterations to the building in the mid-19th century. Their residency was followed by the Van Necks and several short-lived occupants before the place was bought by the Bracknell Development Corporation in 1955. It now houses offices.

Figure 24: The old Running Horse at Bullbrook

Whitegrove was built in the early 1990s, as a Bracknell suburb in Warfield parish. It is named after the small copse that is still there off Harvest Ride. Its original name of Warfield Green is said to have been chosen as an ironic play on the slogan popular with anti-development protestors who wanted to 'keep Warfield green'. An old name for the area, however, was Edmund's Green, a small medieval or Tudor hamlet based around Jigs Lane South.

Burchett's Green and Stubbings

The border between the parishes of Bisham (east) and Hurley (west) passes right through the centre of Burchett's Green. The name is derived from the Byrchet family who are recorded in the area as early as 1284.

Hall Place, nearby, has been the home to the Berkshire College of Agriculture since 1943. It is one of the manors of Hurley, first recorded as 'La Halle' in the 13th century. The estate's earliest surviving features are the avenues of lime trees and the statue of the Roman goddess Diana, laid out for Sir Jacob Bancks, a Swedishman who served with distinction in the British Navy. In 1728, a rich London lawyer, William East, bought the estate and built the core of today's house, although the wings were added later. The Baroque decoration of the garden room is spectacular, with dolphins and cupids and profile busts of Princess Anne (daughter of King George II) and Prince William IV of Orange, whose marriage it celebrates. East's son and namesake was made a baronet and the later family became the Clayton-Easts. Sir East George Clayton-East planted oaks in the park, arranged like the fleets at Nelson's Battle of the Nile.

The name Stubbings is not found before the erection of Stubbings House, now adjoining a garden centre, in 1765. It may be named after the stubs of trees cut down in a partial clearance of Maidenhead Thicket that once spread across this area. The house was the home of Guy Carleton, Lord Dorchester, who was Governor of Quebec and died there in 1808. He had played a prominent role fighting against the American Revolution, successfully holding a besieged Quebec and evacuating the English from New York at the end of the War. The house was extended by Henry Skirne, an Indian tea merchant, who also built the church, in 1850-4, so that his son could be the vicar there. It became the centre of an ecclesiastical parish two years later. The house was also the English home of the exiled Queen Wilhelmina of the Netherlands during the Second World War.

Figure 25: Hall Place at Burchett's Green, built in 1728

Dick Turpin is supposed to have fired several shots at the shutters of the vicarage that he – unfortunately for the story – pre-dated by over a hundred years. This is just one of many stories of local highwaymen active on Maidenhead Thicket. Claude Duval is also said to haunt Burchett's Green; whilst a supposed 'phantom horseman' all in white, who rides the forest lanes around Stubbings and disappears into the Thicket with a thundering of hooves, is said to be the equally notorious Captain Hawkes. Unlike some others, he *is* known to have worked this area, dressing as a farmer, soldier or clergyman to lull his victims into a false sense of security.

Chalvey

Chalvey means Calves' Island, a piece of solid land within the marshes of Slough where cows could be grazed. The original village of Chalvey Green developed around the upper High Street and lower Church Street. Appropriately for its name, the local pound for the parish of Upton-cum-Chalvey was located there, where stray livestock were rounded up.

The manor of Chalvey, based at Manor Farm (on the site of Brammas Close), was owned by the well-known South Buckinghamshire family of Bulstrode until the 18th century. They have several memorial brasses in Upton Church because their main home was Bulstrode Park (aka Hedgerley Bulstrode or Temple Bulstrode), near Gerrards Cross, which was anciently a detached part of Upton-cum-Chalvey parish. In 1718, Chalvey was purchased by Henry Godolphin, Provost of Eton College, who lived at nearby Baylis House, and later passed to his descendants, the Osbornes, who became Dukes of Leeds.

Figure 26: The Story of the Chalvey Stab Monk

A person from Chalvey is traditionally known as a 'Stab Monk'. This stems from an old story that, back in the 1850s, a visiting organ grinder was entertaining the villagers when his monkey, for some reason (perhaps he was provoked), bit a little girl. The father quickly appeared on the scene and stabbed the monkey to death with a kitchen knife. Feeling remorseful, the villagers organised a collection of enough money for both a funeral and an extensive wake. The ceremony was apparently re-enacted every Whit Monday until the First World War, with pall bearers carrying a coloured plaster monkey accompanied by blackened dancing boys. Sometimes a so-called 'Mayor of Chalvey' was elected at the same time.

The Windsor Road on the edge of Chalvey was privately maintained as part of the Colnbrook Turnpike, established in 1727. The old toll house where the toll-keeper collected travellers' money stood on the west side near the Ragstone Road junction. The railway ploughed through the area from 1838 and Chalvey was briefly given its own station but it was not successful and closed after only a year.

Chalvey seems to have always been a poorer area of the 19th century parish. However, it became a home of religious diversity that has lasted to the present day. Amongst those who would not comply with the governance of the Church of England were the Congregationalists who started preaching in Chalvey in 1806, a time when they were still widely persecuted. They built a church in 1835 but moved to Slough in 1852. The Primitive Methodists then took over the building, having arrived a few years before. The Anglicans did not build St Peter's Church until 1860, before which parishioners had to travel all the way to Upton every Sunday. After the arrival of the Asian community in the 1950s, the first purpose built Hindu Temple in Britain was erected in Keel Drive and opened in 1981 after being planned for nearly 20 years. There are also two mosques, one in Ragstone Road and the other in Montem Lane/Arthur Road.

Chavey Down and Winkfield Row

Chavey Down, in Winkfield parish, was the northernmost section of the little-known South Berkshire Moors that stretched from Sandhurst to Bracknell and Ascot. Its most interesting feature was its windmill which is thought to have stood at the junction of Longhill and Priory Roads and Locks Ride. It stood alongside five ancient fishponds and Chavey Down Farm may have been the original miller's house. The mill was certainly there throughout the 18th century and may have been built some considerable time earlier. The place-name probably represents the Chaffing Down where the wheat was separated from the chaff before milling. The area was wild heathland until 1813, when King George III enclosed as much common land as he could get his hands on. He had owned a large portion of Winkfield manor since 1782 and built the present manor house, south of Forest Road, four years later as a royal hunting lodge.

There are other extant buildings of interest in the area too. The Royal Foresters hotel and restaurant on the London Road started out in the 1840s as an alehouse known as the 'Jim Crow,' a politically incorrect 'blacked-up' theatrical character popular at the time. He was featured on the pub sign along with his motto, "Black Boy Dancin': Wheel about and turn-about and do just so. Every time I jump around, I shout Jim Crow." The name was remembered in the segregation laws of the Southern States of America.

Now a spiritual retreat, Ascot Priory was founded near Chavey Down in 1861 and built from 1879 by Reverend Doctor Edward Bouverie-Pusey, from Pusey near Wantage, the promoter of the Anglo-Catholic Oxford Movement. It was the home of the

Society of the Most Holy Trinity, the first religious order founded in the Church of England since the Reformation.

Figure 27: Winkfield Row about 1910

Heathfield was built as a private house in the late 18th century but turned into a girls' school by Miss Eleanor Wyatt in 1899. Royal pupils have included Princesses Olga and Alexandra of Greece and Princess Alexandra, Lady Ogilvy and the present Countess of Snowdon.

Most of the land at Chavey Down was sold off for development in order to pay the owner's debts. The first houses were built in 1879, St Martin's Church five years later, and the village grew rapidly from there. The area called Mushroom Castle developed on common-land where shack-type houses were built overnight to prevent the land being claimed by the Crown. They popped up like mushrooms. Nearby were Page's greenhouses, famous in the 1930s and 40s, for growing carnations, such as the 'Ascot White,' for the London markets. Hence the Carnation Hall and the road names of the adjoining estate. Irises were grown along the Forest Road.

Winkfield Row originally stretched out along Forest Road, but, by the mid-18th century, had extended up the triangle around the old White Horse pub (now an Italian restaurant). The Primitive Methodist Chapel was built in this area in 1854 and St Mary's School was transferred nearby, from near the parish church, in 1862. There used to be a little iron church, built in 1896, alongside, but this was demolished in 1972. There are a number of prominent country houses in the area. Lambrook Hall (1853), a private preparatory school for boys since 1860, has been attended by many a son of the rich and famous, including the sons of Prince Christian of Schleswig-Holstein and Princess Helena (Queen Victoria's daughter) and also of Prime Minister Herbert Asquith. William Sellar and Robert Yeatman, who wrote the classic historical spoof '1066 and All That' in 1931, were also pupils there and tradition has it that work was based on their old history lessons. Lambrook appeared in the manor court rolls as a croft belonging to a certain John Bowyer as early as 1440. The family were farmers at Moss End in Warfield for many generations before returning to Winkfield Row Farm in the early years of the 20th century. Harry Bowyer is well remembered for the extraordinary scrapyard he kept there until his death in 1987.

Cheapside

The Virginia Water is partly in the Cheapside area of Northern Sunninghill parish. It was created by the Duke of Cumberland, the Ranger of Windsor Forest who lived at Cumberland Lodge, in 1753. It had previously been a tiny stream which fed Sunninghill Mill. In the 1790s, King George III proposed erecting a boat house on Sunninghill common land, on the edge of the lake, but he faced considerable opposition because this was an area with a large number of residents.

Cheapside had become established as a small hamlet, just to the west of the mill, by the late medieval period. Its earliest name was Mill Green and the people of Sunninghill parish came to live there because it bordered both common grazing land on the green and the agricultural strips divided amongst them. The name 'cheap' may refer to the poor of the parish, but it can also refer to an innkeeper. 'The Tun' was a very early pub there, dating from at the 1690s and probably earlier. It was later joined by the Thatched Tavern and, by the mid-18th century, Cheapside contained about a third of the parish's population, because there had been much displacement from the Silwood estate.

Figure 28: Sunninghill Park before the fire in 1947

Sunninghill Park, to the north-west, was part of Windsor Forest and the monarch kept a hunting lodge there. Records show Prince Arthur, the eldest son of King Henry VII, staying there in 1499 and his brother, King Henry VIII, holding a royal council there in 1542. King Charles I sold the estate, in 1630, to the Honourable Thomas Carey, a younger son of the Earl of

Monmouth who was Groom of the Royal Bedchamber. The old house was a late Georgian stucco building but, in 1947, whilst being prepared as a home for the newly married Princess Elizabeth (the present queen), it burnt down. In 1990, it was rebuilt, on a new site (over the Winkfield border), in very modern style as a home for the Duke of York but has since been demolished.

Nearby are other great houses. The late 18th century Buckhurst Park, extensively remodelled in the late 20th century, was purchased by King Hussein of Jordan in 1986 and is currently Queen Noor's English home. Harewood House (aka Harewood Lodge aka Sunninghill House) was named by Jane, Lady Harewood (died 1813) in 1806, but the present building, with its hipped and balustraded roof, was built as recently as 1936 by Sir Charles Shaw baronet who had moved there from Charters in Sunningdale. Titness Park (aka Tilney House) was an early 19th century Tudor-Gothic revival house, built for Rear Admiral Sir Home Riggs Popham. He fought in the French Revolutionary and Napoleonic Wars, as well as retaking the Cape of Good Hope from the Dutch. He is also remembered for developing a signalling code for the Navy. The house was totally rebuilt in 1990.

Cippenham

Cippenham Liberty (like a large manor) was historically the south-east portion of the Buckinghamshire parish of Burnham. It became part of Berkshire in 1974. Roman barns have been excavated on the site of the Western House Academy but 'Cippa's Home' was first established in Anglo-Saxon times. Before 1066, it consisted of 8 hides of land farmed by just 6 villeins (tenant farmers), 1 border (cottage dweller) and their families. The manor was tenanted by Edric of Marlow, Saewulf, who also held land in Iver, and Wulfric the Thegn, whose estates were mostly around Levendon in North-West Buckinghamshire. At the time of the Domesday Survey (1086), it belonged to Westminster Abbey.

Figure 29: 17th century Long Barn of Cippenham Court Farm

The village later became known as Cippenham Green as it covered the area around the existing village green, along Mercian Way and Lower Cippenham Lane up to the bend at the Brook Path junction. Most of the houses were concentrated at this junction, in the Warner Close area around Cippenham House, and on the south and east sides of the green itself. Some buildings in this area bear the date 1699, including two brick and timber cottages that were once the Jolly Gardener Inn. Outlying country houses developed along the eastern reaches of Lower Cippenham Lane: Cippenham Place, Court and Lodge. Hidden away to the west of Autumn Close is Cippenham Place, a mid-16th-century timber-framed house with brick infill, enlarged in the 19th century. It had a large moat, the western arm of which still survives. The 17th century Long Barn from Cippenham Court Farm is now a pub and restaurant. Cippenham

Lodge is a beautiful mid-18th century brick house with a large hipped roof that is now a Market Research Viewing Studio at the corner of Weekes Drive and Cippenham Lane.

The area around the Earl of Cornwall pub was originally called Farnham End because it was at the southern tip of old Farnham Royal parish. At the park, down the end of Telford Drive, near a large supermarket, is Cippenham Moat. This is a now dry moat and all that remains of the palace of Prince Richard, Earl of Cornwall, the younger brother of King Henry III: hence the name of the pub. For the rights to this manor, he had to present a pair of golden spurs to the De Ferrers family; but the Earl claimed extensive rights beyond those of a normal manor, including the right to erect and make use of a gallows. In 1231, when he was 22, Richard secretly married the widowed Countess of Gloucester, against his brother's wishes. They spent their honeymoon at Cippenham Palace, nervously awaiting the King's reaction, but luckily he soon forgave them. Richard was later elected King of Germany (aka King of the Romans or Holy Roman Emperor) in 1256. He was crowned in Aachen but rarely left England. He signed the foundation charter for Burnham Abbey at his Cippenham palace in 1266. Doubt has, however, been cast on the 1314 or 1325 record of King Edward II travelling to Cippenham on a barge that had previously delivered faggots to the Royal Court. The associated deer park was later used by King Edward III as a stud farm to provide horses for his French wars.

In December 1645, during the Civil War, some of Cromwell's soldiers were quartered at Burnham. Lieutenant Ryder and "diverse others of his troopers [were] found tippling in a very debase manner" and refused to pursue a royalist cavalry party from Oxford when they carried off two men and weapons from Cippenham.

Clewer Green and St Leonard's Hill

Figure 30: The Clewer House of Mercy, dedicated to St. John the Baptist

Clewer Green was an area of common grazing land, south of Clewer Hill Road, historically used by the Clewer parishioners. It was there, that the widowed King Henry VII met Philip the Handsome, King of Castile (in Spain) and Duke of Burgundy in January 1506. The latter had been summoned to the Royal Court at Windsor Castle after he and his wife had been shipwrecked on the Dorset Coast whilst on their way from Spain to the Netherlands. Philip was somewhat anxious about the meeting, being uncertain of King Henry's motives. In the event, everything was very amicable. Philip was made a Knight of the Garter, but he did sign a number of English-biased treaties in return.

Clewer manor was owned by largely absentee landlords in the 17th and 18th centuries. A new manor house called Clewer Cottage was probably built for the Vansittarts shortly before they sold it off to a certain Richard Foster in 1812 – although they only sold the house and kept the manor and its rights. The present Clewer Manor House on the site was built for Edmund Foster in 1841 and aggrandized in the Jacobean style twenty years later. It eventually became Haileybury School and is now apartments.

When, in 1848, Widow Tennant from Clewer was made aware of the plight of local women caught up in poverty and prostitution, she began to provide them with shelter in her home. This eventually became an Anglican nunnery called the Clewer House of Mercy, or the Community of St John Baptist. At its height, the order had some forty-five different sites around the World and they are still very active in America. The prominent buildings built around three quadrangles in Hatch Lane by Henry Woodyer, between 1853 to 1881, are now flats however. The nuns moved out to Oxfordshire in 2001.

The St Leonard remembered by the hill now named after him, on the edge of Clewer Green, is said locally not to have been named after the well-known 6th century Frankish hermit, but a local holy man. Like his namesake, he was a recluse and resided in a cell, next to a chapel, which he had built for himself on the top of the hill. The first record to survive of this hermitage dates from 1215. It continued in use until the Dissolution, after which only the field name Eremytescroft or Hermit's Croft remained. The hermitage stood on the site of what is now the mansion on the Legoland estate, still called St Leonard's. The associated Holy Well was the spring that feeds the pond there. This was the site of the lost Domesday village (1086) of Losfield (probably a contraction of Leo[nard]'s Field).

Figure 31: St Leonard's Hill: The 1872 Gothic mansion of Lord de Barry

The chapel was mentioned by Sir Thomas Malory in connection with King Arthur and his Knights of the Round Table. He claimed St Leonard's successor to have been one Sir Brastias. He was originally a knight of Duke Gorlois of Tintagel, the man with whose wife, Igraine, King Uther had fallen in love. Merlin magically turned Uther into the image of Gorlois and his bodyguard, Sir Ulfius, into Sir Brastias, so they could steal into Gorlois' castle. Uther was there able to seduce Igraine and thus Arthur, their son, was born. Sir Brastias served Uther, after Gorlois' death, but later retired to the Clewer Hermitage. Many years later, Sir Lancelot took to hiding out there during his turbulent affair with Queen Guinevere. He once visited Sir Lavaine nearby, while training for a tournament. It was not a happy time however. Lancelot fell asleep by St Leonard's Well, just as a lady and her hunting party arrived chasing a hind. She immediately shot the poor knight in the buttocks and rode off. The hermit spent many days nursing Lancelot back to health.

The famous lamp dug up on the site, and used by the Society of Antiquaries as their logo, is now thought to have belonged to the medieval hermit rather than previous Roman inhabitants. However, the ultimate origins of the chapel could still lie in this earlier period, for other Roman remains have been found on the hill. Dedications to St Leonard are often found in wooded areas. Some historians think they indicate where ancient pagan sites connected with the horned Romano-Celtic god of the countryside, Cernnunos, have been converted for Christian worship. This character may be connected with Malory's lady huntress, but his association with Windsor Forest is better attested by his appearance in local folklore as Herne the Hunter, a hunt-leading ghost who supposedly haunts the Great Park.

In later years, the hill became the site of a royal hunting lodge, but, by 1756, this became a private estate and the country retreat of William Pitt, who later became the Earl of Chatham. In the 1770s, the house was purchased by the widowed Countess Waldegrave, daughter of Edward Walpole of Frogmore House. She called it Forest Lodge until she was able to get her secret marriage to King George III's brother, the Duke of Gloucester, accepted by Parliament, when it became Gloucester Lodge. The magnificent estate became known as St Leonard's Hill under the 3rd Earl Harcourt and a new and extraordinary gothic style mansion was built by Lord de Barry in 1872. Unloved by later generations, it was partly pulled down in 1926 and the remains fell into ruin, some of which still survive.

Clewer Village and New Town

The name derives from Clifwara meaning Cliff-Dwellers, i.e. those who lived below the hill on which Windsor Castle was built. The castle site was actually in Clewer manor until acquired by William the Conqueror for his new residence. Clewer Church is said to be the oldest building in Windsor, dating from 1100 or before. Its font is certainly of Anglo-Saxon date. The Brocas Chapel there was founded by the Black Prince's great friend, Sir Bernard Brocas of Clewer Brocas Manor, in 1384. It is a memorial to his wife, Mary, who brought him the hereditary position of Master of the Royal Buckhounds. The hermits of nearby St Leonard's Chapel appear to have been the chantry priests.

Figure 32: Clewer Village predates Windsor

A few other ancient buildings survive in the village: The Limes is a fine 16th century timber-framed house with a brick frontage of 1700; Edgeworth House dating from 1707 was a youth hostel until 2005; and the millhouse, standing near the site of a

Domesday mill (1086), was built when the previous structure burnt down in 1781.

Clewer was a popular spot to build Victorian villas before it joined up with Windsor. Clewer Park, adjoining the mill, was the home of Daniel Gooch, the Victorian industrialist and railway engineer who was responsible for the first transatlantic cables. The house was used by the Wrens during the Second World War but was demolished and the park built upon in the 1950s. Only the gatepiers survive in Maidenhead Road and the striped brick estate cottages on the north side of Mill Lane, dated 1869.

Clewer New Town developed around the Three Elms Crossroads of Dedworth Road/Clarence Road and Hatch Lane/Parsonage Lane. The last road ran from the village to the Parsonage (or Glebe Land, later called the Rectory) in the north-west corner of the junction. It was rebuilt slightly further north by the 1850s and was joined by Bexley Villa – named after the Chancellor of the Exchequer. The manor of Clewer had been acquired by Lord Bexley's uncle, Arthur Vansittart, in 1719. There are two pubs named after them in Vansittart Road. The last of the Vansittart lords of the manor died in 1859 and left the Clewer estate to his two illegitimate sons, Arthur and Gerald Stovell – to the great consternation of his family who were hitherto totally unaware of the boys' existence. The Stovell brothers soon began to lease out their land for building. The area quickly joined up with Windsor and, in 1894, the eastern part of the parish was made part of the borough as Clewer Within. The model Hawker Hurricane in Alexandra Park remembers its designer Sir Sydney Camm who grew up in the area.

Colnbrook and Brands Hill

Historically, the south side of Colnbrook High Street was in Horton parish, while the north side was in a slightly detached part of Langley Marish. It may have been planned that way in order to share road maintenance and other responsibilities. For Colnbrook developed as the first stopping point out of London on the west side of the Middlesex/Buckinghamshire border bridge. You can still see the boundary marked there today.

Figure 33: The historic Ostrich Inn in Colnbrook

Its beginnings may have been in a single 'hospitium' or hospice – an early inn – run by a certain Anglo-Saxon called Aegelward. Miles Crispin, the lord of Wallingford Castle, gave this to Abingdon Abbey in 1106, after its abbot, Faricius, a famous physician, had provided him with medical assistance. The name 'hospice' is supposed to have become corrupted over time to Ostrich: hence the name of the present inn on the site. The name of the Ostrich Inn is only first recorded in 1624, though the writer, Thomas Deloney, mistakenly referred to the "sign of the crane" in 1612 and the building itself dates back to the early 16th century. Deloney tells an old story of how, back in the 12th century, one of the earliest hosts of the inn was a villain called Jarman. He fitted out a certain room there with a secret trap-door beneath the bed, through which he would tip sleeping travellers into a cauldron of boiling ale and steal their goods, whilst claiming they had left very early the next morning. However, his 60th victim was the famous cloth-merchant, Thomas Cole of Reading. When he went missing, a search party soon discovered his lost horse and then his body in the river. Jarman tried to flee but was quickly brought to justice and hanged in the Forest. A similar story is told of the Hind's Head Inn in Bracknell.

Figure 34: Stage coaches were once a common sight in Colnbrook

The oldest building in Brands Hill is the Queen's Arms pub. Is it the same building or an earlier one that appears alone on Rocque's Map of 1761? It was not joined by more houses until the mid-19th century. As the Crown Inn, it was certainly there by 1753 and was probably always surrounded by Spital Farm in its early days. This place seems to have acquired its name from a medieval hospital on the site. It was established before 1442 and may have been connected with Abingdon Abbey's hospice. A later 'cripple house' was built in 1625 at Hermitage Green, on the site of the later Golden Cross Inn (and now the petrol station), at the western end of Colnbrook High Street.

With the formation of the Bristol (later Bath) Road through Colnbrook, the hospice was soon joined by other inns like the Catherine Wheel (now gone but established before 1479), where Henry VIII stayed, and the George (before 1558), where his daughter, Elizabeth I, stayed. As early as 1337, the French ambassadors spent the night in Colnbrook after having met with Edward III at Windsor; while the Jesuit, St Edmund Campion, stopped there under arrest in 1581. It was at Colnbrook that his gaoler received orders not to treat him honourably, but to bind him and display his crimes on a note on his hat; and, thus, he continued to torture and death in London.

The number of inns long outstripped both Maidenhead and Slough and were so well-appointed that they were popular with great men and ladies, not only for accommodation, but for meetings and gatherings outside the capital. In 1265, after the royal victory at the Battle of Evesham at the end of the 2nd Barons' War, the rebel-supporting Londoners had sent a deputation to Colnbrook to come to terms with King Henry III through his representative, Sir Roger Leybourne. Nearly 400 years later, during the Civil War, after the Battle of Edgehill in 1642, Parliament sent (unsuccessful) peace proposals to King Charles I at Colnbrook. It was a place where soldiers would often stop on the march from London to Windsor. Press gangs would gather naval recruits there, bare-knuckle boxing matches were held there and early nonconformists preached there.

Colnbrook was given a charter and made a borough in 1544, with the right to hold a market every Tuesday and two annual fairs. This was confirmed in 1635 when it became administered by a bailiff and 12 burgesses. Perhaps it was these new revenue streams that allowed the 'town' to survive the plague spread from Horton in 1629, the billeting of unruly parliamentary soldiers during the Civil War and the sacking of the town by Prince Rupert's troops after they lost the Battle of Brentford (1642). Earlier, after the failure of the Epiphany Rising to assassinate Henry IV at Windsor, the rebel Earls had considered fortifying Colnbrook but it was saved when they decided to hold the bridge at Maidenhead instead.

Stage coaches were passing through Colnbrook by the 1650s and the Bath Road there was greatly improved by the Colnbrook Turnpike Trust in 1727. The bridge was rebuilt in brick five years later. Most coaches changed horses at Colnbrook by the 1750s and 20 years later, the George was running its own 'Bath and Bristol Diligence' Coach. Mail coaches arrived in the 1810s. This was a golden age for Colnbrook. However, in 1832, the Reform Act took away its borough status and, with the arrival of the Railway in the area, the town's decline began.

In 1830, a retired brewer, called Richard Cox, developed the Cox's Orange Pippin and other apples at the Lawns (aka Colnbrook Lawn). Unfortunately, however, he died before it became the well-known fruit it is today. A memorial orchard now stands on the site of Cox's house on the corner of Albany Park, with Pippins Park not far away.

Colnbrook had had a small chapel, originally a chantry chapel, since 1342. This was joined by a Baptist Church in 1745 and a

Methodist Church in 1850. An Anglican parish church was built in 1853. The village was united with Iver parish in 1894 and most of the northern part of modern Colnbrook was historically part of Iver. Colnbrook joined with Poyle and became part of Berkshire in 1995.

Cookham

Figure 35: The Tarry Stone in the middle of Cookham High Street

Stone Age people lived on Winter Hill in the northern reaches of the parish and, in the Bronze Age, were buried under round barrows still to be seen on nearby Cock Marsh. Badly excavated in the 1870s, they revealed the burials of a cremated woman, a cremated child and a small horse. An important Iron Age find from the parish, now in the British Museum, is an iron dagger with ornate copper-alloy butterfly-shaped hilt and sheath with (missing) red coral studs. The Romans appear to have had some sort of settlement at the southern end of the village. This was approximately at the junction of the Roman roads known as the Camlet Way and Alderman Silver's Road. The place may have been a villa, though the main building has not yet been discovered. Finds of quern stones and agricultural implements certainly imply a farming community, as do two impressive corn-drying facilities

The Camlet Way ran from St Albans to Silchester and appears to have crossed the Thames at Sashes Island in Cookham. Wooden piles and stakes found there in the 19th century (and again in 1969) may indicate the remains of a substantial bridge. There was probably an adjoining river port named Cwch-ium – Celtic for Boat-Place (the alternative Anglo-Saxon Cook's Home seems somewhat obscure). The earliest Anglo-Saxon settlers in the parish appear to have liked the area around Cookham Rise, but later they moved towards the river. The island of Odney may have been sacred to the chief Anglo-Saxon god, Woden: 'Od'n-ey meaning Woden's Isle. Nearby Sashes Island eventually became one of King Alfred's burhs, a fortified place of refuge built for use during periods of Viking invasion.

Figure 36: Frederick Walker's memorial in Cookham Church

The present village of Cookham probably mostly took off in the 8th century after an Anglo-Saxon monastery was founded there.

It was probably a twin-house for both monks and nuns. A national religious synod once met there. The old abbey church is probably the basis of the present parish church which shows signs of Anglo-Saxon work in the chancel. It certainly became an Anglo-Saxon Minster in later years. The kings of Wessex also had a 'Royal Vill' or intermittent palace next door, where the Witan (Anglo-Saxon parliament) met in AD 997. This probably stood in Little Berry Field.

The present church is mostly 13th century, but there is an interesting Lady Chapel closely dated to 1182. It was built on the site of a hermitage that adjoined the old Norman building. An anchoress lived there through the generosity of King Henry II, who may have been trying to expiate himself for the murder of St Thomas Becket in his name. She died in 1181 and was probably buried in the Norman style grave found just outside the walls. There were less virtuous inhabitants interred in the churchyard in later centuries. The parish register contains the following entry:

March 9th 1741,
Richard Smith, a highwayman shot on the road.

There are several good brasses in the church. One is to Edward Woodyer (1613) whose home, Churchgate House, adjoins the churchyard. This old timber-framed house was originally built around 1350. It has a priest-hole and is said to have been the residence of the Abbot of Cirencester. Though this man was officially the village rector, he was probably rarely seen there. The extent of Cirencester Abbey's property was said to be marked by the Tarry Stone (or Cookham Stone) that now stands at the end of the High Street but was originally in the middle of the road junction just opposite. This is a very mundane explanation for the presence of a fascinating object. It is an old sarsen stone, not native to the area, which may indicate some ancient religious significance, perhaps remembered in the village games that were once played around it.

The 19th century artist, Frederick Walker, lived in Cookham, near the Bel and Dragon. His best-known work is 'The Bathers' [at Cookham] that so inspired his fellow artists at the Royal Academy, including Sir John Millais. Cookham is most famous, however, as the home of Stanley Spencer who lived in the village for many years and several of his paintings – notably 'The Resurrection, Cookham' – were set there. His grave can be seen in the churchyard and the village even has its own art gallery dedicated to his memory. It is housed in the old Methodist Chapel in which he once worshipped.

Kenneth Grahame wrote the 'Wind in the Willows' at Cookham Dean and the character of Mr Toad was inspired by the eccentric Colonel Francis Ricardo of Lullebrook House (now the Odney Club and perhaps the original 'Toad Hall') on Odney Island. He was the Sheriff of Berkshire in 1894 and 1913 and the first person in Cookham to own a car: a canary yellow Rolls Royce Silver Ghost – just like the one that got Mr Toad into so much trouble. Grahame mentions the ford near the old fort on Sashes Island as the place where Otter taught his son, Portly, to swim.

An earlier owner of Lullebrooke House was James Burrows, a retired London leather-merchant. From 1828, he encouraged struggling local cobblers to make high quality ready-made boots and shoes and supplied them with materials and a market. He established a thriving industry around his house, employing 1,500 people (including outworkers). They would all arrive in the village on Fridays with their finished boots carried over their shoulders. The family kept the industry going into the 1880s when cheap competition from the Midlands led to its collapse.

Cookham Dean

Dean is an old word for a valley. Settlements there first grew up around upper Church Road and middle Dean Lane. Between the two is Harding's Green, one of 12 pieces of common land in Cookham parish saved from enclosure. It is supposed to be the site of the burning of a local witch who, when the faggots were lit, had her cat jump on her shoulders and off she flew. This certainly illustrates that this was where some of the earlier inhabitants lived and some of the most interesting old buildings are located around the junction of Dean Lane and Alleyns Lane, just to the north. The old Forge was built in 1532. It became a blacksmith's soon afterwards and remained so for nearly 500 years. The beautiful thatched Cromwell Cottage (once four cottages) is said to have had roundhead soldiers billeted there during the Civil War. It was certainly very convenient for the forge, and it is thought that there was some kind of military skirmish at Cookham Dean Bottom.

Figure 37: Cookham Dean, with Cromwell Cottage in the distance

The place should really be called Great Bradley after the lost manor that covered this area, but now only remembered in the name of Bradcutts Lane. The manor house probably stood just to the north of Cookham Dean, somewhere near the house called Chimneys, along Winter Hill. It was largely owned by absentee landlords, but, for 50 years in the late 17th century, it was owned by the Turberville family from Penllyn Castle near Cowbridge. They seem to have used Bradley as a residence more convenient for London. The Turbervilles were Roman Catholic recusants, constantly obliged to pay fines for following their religion. A memorial hidden away in Cookham Church records how, at the age of only 26, John Turberville was killed fighting for the Catholic King James II against his Protestant son-on-law, William of Orange, near Warminster. This was one of the few battles of the erroneously named 'bloodless' Glorious Revolution of 1688 that brought William to the English Throne. The manor had its own wharf called Bradelhythe, at the end of Stone House Lane. It was originally owned by the monks of Bisham Abbey and it was they who built the old 'stone house' from which to monitor trade there.

Although the Methodists had been the earliest denomination to preach in the area, the Anglican church at Cookham Dean was eventually erected in 1845 and the place became an ecclesiastical parish the following year. The building has two copies in Australia. An unlikely story suggests that a huge elm tree that once stood outside was an important boundary marker for Windsor Forest. One of the curates there was the uncle of the author, Kenneth Grahame. Grahame lived at The Mount in Long Lane with his grandmother and uncle as a child, and later returned to Mayfield, now Herries School, where he consolidated his son's bedtime stories into the 'Wind in the

Willows'. He is thought to have drawn inspiration from many locations in and around Cookham and Bisham.

Cookham Rise

The earliest Anglo-Saxon settlers in Cookham parish appear to have lived near Coxburgh Field (now the Alfred Major Park). Their cemetery has been discovered in what was Noah's Ark Field (ark meaning casket, i.e. coffin), in the Terry's Lane area near the railway. Only later did they move nearer the river to start the present village. However, the medieval High Street at Cookham was never able to extend westward because it terminates at the marshy common land of Cookham Moor – saved from enclosure and now National Trust property. A series of seven narrow and rickety timber walkways used to be the only way across the moor in times of flood. On the far side is the area known as The Pound where the village pound was used to round up stray cattle and sheep. It was to there that the village had already expanded by the mid-18th century, hopping over the Moor completely. These were the beginnings of Cookham Rise.

Figure 38: Hillyers, home of both Grahame and Marconi

The railway station was built in 1854 and housing was developed along High and Lower Roads, stretching to the west, soon afterwards. The house called Meliora, now gone but the home of the Kings in High Road, was painted by their friend, Stanley Spencer, several times when he spent his later years at Cliveden View, just to the south. Hillyers, at the corner of Whyteladyes Lane, was briefly rented to Kenneth Grahame before he moved to Cookham Dean. It was then taken on, in 1896, by Doctor Sir Leander Starr Jameson, the man who helped spark the Boer War by technically invading the Transvaal. He had investigated the use of 'wireless telegraphy' in Africa for Cecil Rhodes, and so invited his cousin, Guglielmo Marconi to stay. The latter conducted some of the earliest radio wave experiments from the garden and is believed to have tried to send transmissions across the Thames.

The major expansion of the Rise did not occur until the 1950s and 60s, but it lost one prominent building in 1968. The Pound had boasted a late 19th century concrete folly studded with old glass bottles, pebbles, fossils and reputedly even Iron Age weapons dredged from the lake on the Moor. It was named Strande Castle after the stream, but had no reinforcement, became unsafe and had to be demolished.

Cox Green

The Thames Valley is not best known for its luxurious Roman villas, but the finest one discovered in Berkshire so far, lies under the western end of Northumbria Avenue. It was fully excavated in 1959 when a standard winged-corridor type villa was revealed, which was occupied between the 2nd and 4th centuries. The owners did not spend their money on luxuries like patterned mosaics, but instead were intent on having the latest comforts: like underfloor heating and an elaborate Roman bath suite with hot steam room and cold plunge pool.

Cox Green encompasses two major attractively named medieval manor houses of the old parish of Bray. They sit right next to one another in Ockwells Road: Lillibrooke and Ockwells. The present Lillibrooke Manor is a timber-framed farmhouse-style brick building, put up about 1490 for the Martyn family from Dorset, possibly so they could be within easy reach of the Royal Court at Windsor. Then around 1541, it was purchased as a, rather distant, dower house to Englefield House, near Reading.

Figure 39: Ockwells Manor, built in 1450

Ockwells has more magnificence. It is "the most refined and sophisticated late medieval timber-framed house in England". It was built, in about 1450, for Sir John Norreys, the Master of the Royal Wardrobe who controlled King Henry VI's personal expenditure, and access to the King himself, during the Wars of the Roses. Norreys had the windows of the hall filled with expensive stained glass, which still survives today, showing the coats of arms of all his Lancastrian friends. This became rather embarrassing when the Yorkists came to power and he quickly had to change sides. After Sir John's death, his widow married the man who was to become the first Howard Duke of Norfolk and the two often stayed at Ockwells. Norfolk was great friends with King Richard III and was the man who persuaded Queen Elizabeth Woodville to give up her son, the Duke of York, from sanctuary in Westminster Abbey to become one of the vanishing 'Princes in the Tower'. Ockwells was later the childhood country seat of Sir Henry Norreys, whose supposed affair with Queen Anne Boleyn led to both their executions. William Morris founded the Society for the Protection of Ancient Buildings (SPAB) to secure the building's future, after it had been threatened with demolition in 1877.

The settlement of Cox Green itself seems to have been first established as an early kind of almshouse in the 1620s. The name was in use from about 1800, but who exactly Mr Cox was is unknown. The area between Cox Green and Tittle Row was occupied by Maidenhead Race Course, sometimes attended by King George II and the Royal family, from the 1750s until about 1810. By the mid-19th century the area had become a small village with its own pub, called the Foresters, but most of the expansion of housing happened after the Second World War.

Cranbourne and Woodside

Cranbourne is split between the parishes of Winkfield and Windsor. The village is in the former and Cranbourne Chase or Walke is in the latter. The Chase was one of the sixteen sub-divisions of Windsor Forest and not part of the adjoining Great Park. It was unusual for its fallow as opposed to the more usual red deer. The home of the Keeper was called Cranbourne Lodge, better known today as the Cranbourne Tower. This office dates back to, at least, the reign of Henry IV, though the lodge was first built by Henry VII. The present building is mostly late Georgian.

Figure 40: Cranbourne Tower showing the demolished Lodge

Thomas Warde was appointed Keeper in 1535. He was also Porter of the Outer Gate of Windsor Castle and, in 1543, he saved the Protestant activist, Robert Testwood, from an attack by one of the royal canons, prior to him being burnt to death as one of the Windsor Martyrs. Warde's son later became lord of the manor of nearby Winkfield (and Hurst). King James II's first wife, Anne Hyde, was born in the Lodge; and Samuel Pepys had an awkward meeting there with his commander, Sir George Carteret, when acting as a naval messenger. He first got lost in Windsor Forest, then, when he eventually arrived, he found the Lodge under reconstruction. Pepys had to climb up a ladder to Sir George's bedroom, the only room in use. The knight was still in bed and was not amused by the news of an English defeat off Norway.

Adjoining the Chase is the estate of Fernhill. In the 18th century, it was the last Berkshire home of the ancient Knollys family, descendants of Sir Francis Knollys, Treasurer of Queen Elizabeth I's royal household. In the 1760s, it was the home of Roger Drake, the Governor of Calcutta and President of Bengal before Clive of India. When Drake refused to stop increasing British defences at Fort William in Calcutta, the local Nabob besieged the place and captured it. Though Drake escaped, the British who were left behind were thrown into a very small gaol called the 'Black Hole of Calcutta,' where a large number of them died in the night from suffocation and heat exhaustion. In the 1820s, Fernhill Park also became the British residence of Lord Metcalfe, the Governor General of India, who is buried in Winkfield parish church.

An adjoining 18th century mansion, Cranbourne Court, was once part of the same estate. It has had various names over the years and a myriad of well-known residents, including the Victorian actress Edna May and singer Rod Stewart. Bob Hope rented it in the Summer of 1961 when filming 'The Road to Hong Kong' and lived there with Bing Crosby and their respective families.

Slightly nearer the village is Lovel Hill House. In origin, it is a Queen Anne House. Its most famous resident was the scientist and inventor, Admiral Sir Charles Knowles, an illegitimate relative of the Knollyses. The hamlet of Woodside developed along the eastern edge of the Lovel Hill estate in the late 18th century. Both the Rose and Crown and the Duke of Edinburgh pubs there appear to date from the 1870s.

Figure 41: Cranbourne Hall shortly before demolition

The earliest settlement in this area may have been the place called Naldens that appears on Norden's 1607 map of Windsor Forest. It may have stood around the Old Hatchet pub. Cranbourne village itself developed as two parallel settlements named after the tracks along which the houses were built: North Street and Hatchet Lane. They were eventually joined up at their western ends by what is officially called Plaistow Green along Lovel Road. The brick primary school there, with attractive cupola, was built in 1880 as Cranbourne Ranelagh School (which was extended by the opening of a Ranelagh grammar school in Bracknell in 1908). Nearby is Kilbees Farm, or Manor (1590), the ancient home of the Montague family who have a fine brass in Winkfield Church to one of their number who was a Yeoman of the Guard (similar to a Beefeater). An arrow kept at the farm for many years was said to have been the one that gave the place its name. It was presented, by Queen Elizabeth I, to one of the Montagues after an extraordinary feet of archery in which he shot this straight into a hive of bees.

Other important houses in the area include Orchard Lea of 1884, the home of the pre-First World War army reformer, Viscount Esher and his family (his daughter, Lady Brooke, was the last Ranee of Sarawak in Malaysia); and the late 17th century Winkfield Place where Constance Spry's cookery college began; There is also the Pump Room at the end of Winkfield Lane, dating from about 1800 when Cranbourne had its own spa. It was built above a healing well, now covered over. The upper storey of the porch, opening out onto the full-height pump room, was designed to accommodate a small orchestra: one can imagine the merriment that occurred. The aforementioned Ranelagh School was first founded by the Earl of Ranelagh in 1709 as the Green School at the recently demolished Cranbourne Hall.

Crowthorne

The Crow Thorn was originally a local landmark on Circle Hill amongst the moorland which covered this part of Windsor Forest. It stood at the junction of the Devil's Highway (the Roman road from London to Silchester) and the Sandhurst to Bracknell Road – now called Brooker's Corner. By 1823, there were two dwellings nearby and one survives today as Edgbarrow Cottage. It was then a roadside tearoom.

This minute settlement was considerably enlarged in the Victorian Age when the famous college and hospital were both built and the employees needed nearby homes. The Railway

Station was added in 1860 and a wooden church in 1868. Although this was later put on rollers and moved across the road to serve as a corn store when the present church was erected in 1872 at a cost of £1,934-19s. By 1894, when the area had its own parish carved out of Sandhurst, it had become the 'new town' of its time and there was a proposal to call the place Albertville after Prince Albert. Luckily, however, Doctor Edward White Benson, led a successful campaign to retain the ancient name. There is no truth in the old legend that his wife made the title up, after seeing a crow sitting on a thorn tree.

Figure 42: Early photograph of the recently demolished Waterloo Hotel

Doctor Benson was the first headmaster of Wellington College and later became Archbishop of Canterbury. His sons, AC Benson who wrote the words to 'Land of Hope and Glory' and EF Benson who was the author of the Mapp and Lucia novels, were both born at the college. Built between 1856 and 1859 at Kitt Holk's Bottom through a public subscription of £145,000, the school was designed in an 18th century French chateau style by John Shaw, with a chapel by Gilbert Scott. It was one of two national memorials to the 1st Duke of Wellington in the local area. Queen Victoria's son, Prince Alfred, laid the foundation stone and he was, thus, for many years remembered in the name of one of the town's pubs (now just the Prince). Wellington was originally supposed to be a school for the orphans of British officers. Though its range of pupils has expanded, it is still one of the best-known public schools in the country.

Figure 43: French chateau style Wellington College, completed in 1859

This was a highly appropriate place for siting the College, for the Iron Duke used to enjoy hunting in the area: hence the name of Duke's Ride. It should be remembered that much of the modern town, north of this road, lies over the border in Wokingham Without and would best be referred to as Bigshotte. Bigshotte Lodge stood on the site of Norwood's Ravenswood Village. It was the centre of Bigshotte Walke, one of the sixteen portions into which Windsor Forest was split. Bigshotte 'Rayles' were nearby, an enclosed area of railings built by the King for herding red deer. It was in Bigshotte Park that, while out hunting with King George III, the horse of a certain Mr Parry caught its foot in a rabbit hole and sent him head over heels. Landing on his head, he was dreadfully disfigured "without the least sign of life," until Doctor Taplin from Wokingham bled him and, much to the King's delight, he recovered at once. The name of the park was long remembered at Bigshotte School, a bit further along the Nine Mile Ride. The boundary of this region actually follows the old Devil's Highway, just north of the ride.

The infamous high-security psychiatric hospital at Crowthorne is, of course, Broadmoor. It was founded in 1863, after much campaigning by the Earl of Shaftesbury. Safety considerations led to it being located on Lodge Hill in, what was then, a remote region of the Berkshire Moors. In the first seven years, there were some fifteen escapes and it was decided to raise the perimeter wall by sixteen and a half feet. Fortunately, security has improved somewhat since then.

Following the building of Wellington and Broadmoor, Crowthorne Hight Street began to grow up on the edge of Pine Hill which was originally called Small Brook Moor. The Berkshire Moors are a largely forgotten yet unique part of the county's natural landscape. Although much built upon, they still survive in part and can be best viewed on foot, or whilst travelling along the Crowthorne By-Pass from Sandhurst to Bracknell. This area is the real Broad Moor, sometimes called Broad Moor Bottom, but there were, and are, other moors spreading across the old parish of Sandhurst and into

Easthampstead and Winkfield. The area was part of Windsor Forest, a popular royal hunting ground. Near the site of the Transport Research Laboratory, at the northern end of Buckler's Forest, is Clay Hill which was once called Standing Hill. It had such a good view of the area that a 'standing' (or spectator stand) was erected there, in the Elizabethan era, from which the ladies of the court, including the Queen herself on occasion, could watch the deer being hunted.

In the 17th and 18th centuries, this wide expanse of open moorland also became notorious for a different kind of sport. It was a place well known to be frequented by highwaymen. One was apparently a local man, Parson Darby from Yateley or Eversley, just over the border in Hampshire, although his existence is now disputed. He was said to have preached on Sundays and robbed unfortunate travellers in the week. His stable-boy could never understand why this quiet parson's horse was always so tired. Darby was eventually caught and hanged after shooting the Royal Mail's coachman on Bagshot Heath.

Datchet

Datchet, originally in Buckinghamshire, became part of Berkshire in 1974. The name is an unusual Celtic survival in the area, meaning the Best Wood. Interestingly, there was an Iron Age farmstead south of the village and similarly dated Celtic metalwork has been found in and near the Thames at Datchet. Notable examples are an amber and blue glass decorated brooch and a fine spearhead with tiny applied bronze spiral and trumpet patterned panels. The former can be seen at Eton College and the latter in the British Museum. The spear was probably ceremonial and was sacrificed to the gods in the same way that

King Arthur had Excalibur thrown into the lake at the end of his life.

The attractive timber-framed 'manor' buildings, on the north side of the Green, date from 1500. They do not actually include the manor house but were part of the wider manorial complex. Datchet's manor house is called Riding Court, a 17th century house north of the village. It was owned by the Dukes of Montagu and Dukes of Buccleuch, but they rented it out to tenants and lived at nearby Ditton Park instead.

Figure 44: Datchet Church and the Royal Stag on the Green

The Green was once mostly covered by a large pool fed by the Linch Field Brook. The 15th century Royal Stag (aka the Bridge House), on the south side, became a pub about 100 years after its construction. It appears in Jerome K Jerome's Three Men in a Boat (1888), along with the Manor Hotel opposite – a 17th century building first licensed in 1753 – as the two places where the party failed to find accommodation. A well-known story tells how a Victorian child froze to death in the adjoining churchyard whilst waiting for their drunken father to leave the

Royal Stag. In the 1970s, the child's ghostly handprint was said to appear on a certain window pane, even after it was replaced, but the spreading of this rumour appears to have been a simple publicity stunt.

Figure 45: Old Bridge House, traditional home of Nell Gwynne

The Royal Stag was given to the village by Queen Elizabeth I so that its revenue could pay for the up-keep of a bridge, over the pool on the Green, which carried the High Street down to the ferry. Today the charity in charge of the building is called the Barker Bridge House Trust after the last of the commissioners, Robert Barker, who, shortly before his death in 1645, made arrangements for the Queen's wishes to carry on. Robert and his father, Christopher (who has a memorial in the church), had been the royal printers who famously produced the authorised version of the King James Bible. They lived at Southlea Manor (now Farm), an old grange of St Helen's Priory in Bishopsgate that once stood within its own hamlet, south of the village towards the Albert Bridge.

Victoria Bridge and Albert Bridge were put up in 1851 to replace the old bridge at the end of the High Street that had been built on the site of the old ferry. For centuries, the ferry was the main Thames crossing between Windsor and London and was used extensively by the monarch and their large entourage. Queen Anne built the first bridge but there were many replacements, each giving rise to arguments over who was liable for repairs.

King Charles II is said to have kept his mistress, Nell Gwynne, at Old Bridge House – at the end of the High Street where the old bridge was – because, when the Queen was at Windsor, she would not have her in the same county. This is certainly a 16th century building, despite its later appearance. Charles II used to come to the island called Black Pots Ait, near the parish boundary, for the fishing and Antonio Verrio, the artist who specialised in magnificent figured ceilings, built him a summer-house there. This had previously been the site of a fishing lodge belonging to the Provost of Eton, Sir Henry Wotton, who was often visited there by his friend, Isaak Walton, the great fisherman.

In the 18th century, the village had an unsavoury reputation and became known as Black Datchet, although there were some more genteel residents. For a while in the 1780s, the astronomers, William and Caroline Herschel, lived at the now-demolished Lawns (later Satis House) in Horton Road.

Ditton Park was historically a detached part of Stoke Poges parish. It included a small hamlet called Ditton Green around Ditton Farm. Both are now part of Datchet but separated from it by the M4 motorway and mostly approached from Langley. In

1331, John Moleyns crenellated his manor house at Ditton and made it a castle, probably digging the fine moat that still survives. Four years later, he was given a licence to empark the surrounding land for hunting deer and also to hold an annual fair on the 15th August. The area became a royal park in 1472 and, in Tudor times, was often used as a home for the young Princess Mary (later Queen Mary Tudor). She would cross the Thames at Datchet Ferry to go and see her father, King Henry VIII, at Windsor Castle. Old Ditton Castle was rebuilt by the keeper and Secretary of State, Sir Ralph Winwood, in the early 17th century. From him, the manor passed to the Dukes of Montagu and, later, the Dukes of Buccleuch, who used it as one of their homes through the 18th and 19th centuries. The present house was built by Elizabeth, Duchess of Buccleuch, after a fire in 1812, but appears to contain some 14th century work and quite a lot of stained glass was saved from the old house.

The Admiralty Compass Observatory took over the park in 1917. On its western edge, was established the Radio Research Station (later called the Appleton Laboratory). Scientific firsts taking place there included the confirmation of the existence of the ionosphere in 1926 and the development of Radar detection by Sir Robert Watson-Watt in 1935. The station later moved into space science but merged with the Rutherford Laboratory and had left the site by 1981.

Dedworth

Dedworth was first established as a small Anglo-Saxon settlement: Dydda's Farm. Dydda was the name of the father of St Frideswide, who was a minor king in the Oxfordshire/Berkshire area in the 7th century. It is unclear if this was the same man, but perhaps he had a palace at Old Windsor and this was an outlying farm providing his court with agricultural produce. By the reign of King Edward the Confessor, the monarch of all England was certainly living at Old Windsor and the small manor of Dedworth had become the home of important royal officials who liked to be near the King. Hugh the Chamberlain was then in residence.

Figure 46: Old Dedworth, separated from Windsor until 1930

After William the Conqueror took power, Dedworth was given to the royal chaplain (and possibly also the royal physician), Albert the Clerk (aka Albert Lothingaria). This man was from Lorraine and had served King Edward but managed to survive the regime change. At the time of the Domesday Survey (1086), Dedworth only covered one hide and was home to just four villeins (tenant farmers) and one bordar (cottage-dweller) and their families. They had two plough teams to work the land and there was enough woodland for five pigs and twenty acres of meadow for grazing down by the River.

The manor soon became part of the parish of Clewer and was divided in two. A now-covered irregular quadrangular moat in Wolf Lane may be all that remains of the manor house of Dedworth Maunsell, named after a branch of the famous Welsh family usually spelt Mansel. The family was certainly there in the early 14th century, and probably before, since the chaplain at Losfield Chapel on St Leonard's Hill in the 1210s was named Robert Mansel.

The other manor house in the area, Dedworth Loring, may possibly have been located further north where a large medieval hearth was uncovered by excavation in the aptly named Knight's Close. It was named after the De Loring (or Loryng) family whose name means 'of Lorraine,' so they were almost certainly descended from Albert the Clerk. Their main country seat was at Chalgrave in Bedfordshire, but they probably stayed in Dedworth when attending the Royal Court. Sir Peter de Loring is recorded there in the early 13th century. His grandson, Sir Nigel, was Chamberlain to the Black Prince and became a founding member of the Order of the Garter. Centuries later, Sir Arthur Conan Doyle made him the titular character in his novel, 'Sir Nigel' (and he previously appeared in the 'White Company'). However, in the late 1340s, both manors were sold up to Sir John Brocas of the adjoining manor of Clewer Brocas. The manor houses may have provided much needed accommodation for younger members of the Brocas family. In 1360, a John de Loring, became a Canon of Windsor, so presumably there were younger branches of this family still living in the area too.

There are streets in Dedworth named after both the Mansel and Loring families. Several others are named after the Windsor

Martyrs who were burnt to death for their Protestant beliefs at the end of King Henry VIII's reign. What their connection with Dedworth was is unclear. They were all Windsor townsmen at a time when Dedworth was a small hamlet of less than ten houses. The small community seems to have had a distinct sense of independence from both Clewer and Windsor. In 1700, they refused to pay poor (or church) rates due to Windsor parish. The situation continued for three years until the Dedworth inhabitants were taken to the Assize Court in Wallingford and forced to pay up. By 1800, there were still only thirteen dwellings in Dedworth, but they housed some seventy-five people, with around six people in each house. The population grew steadily throughout Queen Victoria's reign and was just over 400 by the time of her death (1901).

Figure 47: The old Queen Pub, now closed

Dedworth was given its own church in 1863 – All Saints' – erected by GF Bodley for the Tudor family. It was an Arts-and-Crafts brick structure with a small bellcote in the style of a 14th century building. It was torn down after suffering from subsidence and replaced by the current rather imposing modern building with open tower (now with a rather interesting sculpture) in 1971. Fortunately, the glorious Pre-Raphaelite Morris windows were saved and the new church sports stained-glass by Morris himself, Burne-Jones, Rossetti and Ford Madox Brown. Three years after the construction of the first church, Windsor Racecourse was built at Dedworth. It is one of only two figure-of-eight flat race courses in the Country. The original Windsor Races had been instigated by King Charles II at Datchet Mead in the Home Park, down by the Thames opposite Datchet.

By 1930, Dedworth had more-or-less joined up with Clewer and Windsor, although it was still a small ribbon development with farms and open fields. The eastern region of the parish was filled in during the 1950s and spread westward in the 60s and 70s to form the large expanse of housing that we see today.

Easthampstead and Wildridings

One of the oldest historic sites in Bracknell is Bill Hill, a small rise in the Easthampstead area. A circular mound on its eastern side is what remains of a Bronze Age round barrow surrounded by a single ditch, now barely visible. A dip in the centre suggests it has been disturbed by treasure hunters in centuries past. There is no Westhampstead. Throughout the Norman and medieval periods, the village was always called Yethamstead, meaning Gate [into Windsor Forest] Homestead. The old parish of Easthampstead was always an important place. The local workhouse was based there and the district council was named after it, but it is now just part of the town of Bracknell.

The road, Fountain's Garth in Wildridings, is supposed to have been the site of a holy spring where St Birinus baptised King Cynegils of Wessex after converting him to Christianity at Easthampstead Park in AD 634, although some people think this happened at a well near Easthampstead Church. The story may be of no great age but, if it happened at all, it would have been a very quick ceremony which took place sometime prior to King Cynegils' official baptism at Dorchester-on-Thames.

Figure 48: Burne-Jones' superb east window in Easthampstead Church

The old medieval parish church at Easthampstead was almost entirely rebuilt from 1865-67 for the 4th Marchioness of Downshire from Easthampstead Park, but the present building still retains some interesting fittings, particularly a screen made from panels of a former rood and a 15th century brass to an Eton Scholar. Memorials include one to the poet, Elijah Fenton, tutor to the son of William Trumbull of Easthampstead Park. He translated Homer's 'Odyssey' with Alexander Pope from Binfield, and the latter wrote his epitaph. Another literary great who may have attended the church was the poet, Percy Bysshe Shelley. He certainly lived in Bracknell during 1813 but is also said to have rented Reed Hill Farm in Easthampstead for a while. The church's great treasures are its magnificent set of pre-Raphaelite stained-glass windows by Sir Edward Burne-Jones, particularly the great east window of St Michael: his finest anywhere.

Opposite the church, William Watts of South Hill Park founded an almshouse in 1760. This was replaced by the current building (at the centre of the Church Hill House Mental Health Facility) in 1826 and was extended when it became the Union Workhouse eight years later. The 4th Marquess of Downshire donated the cupola clock in 1847. An old story tells how he had purchased it for the church but gave it away when the rector refused to cut back the yew tree that continually knocked off his top hat on the way to Sunday service.

Not far away, at the foot of the hill, the mill pond is still a prominent and attractive feature of the Easthampstead landscape, but the mill has long gone. A 17th century miller is said to have been so mean to the locals during a time of famine that the mill was cursed, his business failed and the building was eventually burnt down.

William Davies, a well-to-do Gloucestershire farmer, made regular trips to Berkshire, but he didn't reap corn there. He held up the local coaches and took gold from their passengers, always leaving behind their jewels and other valuables. His neighbours always wondered why his bills were paid in gold. Little did they know he was the infamous 'Golden Farmer': a man with something of a Robin Hood reputation. For many a local poor man became accustomed to finding a golden guinea thrust beneath his door on nights when the highwayman had been abroad. The pub in South Hill Road is called the Golden Farmer after him. Some say it stands on the site of an earlier building that William frequented on, what was then, the edge of Gore Moor. However this is probably a confused memory of a watering hole near Bagshot. He was eventually caught and hanged in London. His body was apparently hung in chains next to the old pub wherever it was.

Figure 49: The Golden Farmer

The earliest record of Wildridings dates from 1463. However, this area was further west than the Bracknell suburb of today. It was the name of the woods that is now the site of the Southern Industrial Estate. Only one small patch remains around a little footpath, a haven amongst Waitrose warehouses. The name is Anglo-Saxon: Wid-Ryding meaning Wide Clearing. It fits in well today with the rides through Windsor Forest created for Queen Anne and George III. However, the original name for the present Wildridings area was Walden's Green, a small hamlet around the Green Man pub. A Walden family is recorded in Winkfield in the 16th century.

Easthampstead was the second area of Bracknell New Town to be developed from 1957, including new shops and a 'feature' high rise block of flats – Point Royal – by the same architect who designed the Sydney Opera House. By 1962 over 1,300 houses had been built there. Wildridings was not supposed to be part of the original New Town, but pressure for further housing led to this expansion by 1967. There were to be no shops for another two years.

For Easthampstead Park, see Great Hollands and Jennett's Park.

Eton and Eton Wick

Eton is an Anglo-Saxon name meaning River Town. At the time of the Domesday Survey (1086), it consisted of 15 villeins (tenant farmers), 4 bordars (cottage dwellers), 4 serfs and their families. There was also a fishery producing 200 eels a year and two mills. One of the mills was almost certainly on the site of the mill at the end of Tangier Lane, between Cutler's Ait and Tangier Eyot. The land and the river provided employment at this time, but things changed with the building of the wooden bridge to Windsor. It first appears in the written record in 1172 but was probably put up soon after William the Conqueror chose the place that was to become Windsor to build his castle. There were a number of rebuilds and disputes over repairs until the present bridge was constructed in 1822-24. It was closed to vehicular traffic in 1970. The old ferry once crossed to the Brocas meadow, originally Brocas Toft, named after the lords of Clewer Brocas manor who owned land there from around 1337. Brocas Field was historically held by the rent of a single red rose supplied every St John's Day.

Figure 50: Eton College, founded by King Henry VI in 1440

From the building of the first bridge following the Conquest, the High Street, extending northwards, developed as the main centre of Eton and quickly became lined with businesses serving travellers to Windsor. The right to hold a Monday (later Wednesday) market was granted in 1204 and two annual fairs followed two hundred years later. Inns and alehouses especially thrived in Eton, particularly after the founding of the College in 1440 which brought so many visitors to the village. Notable is the Christopher Hotel which is named after the patron saint of travellers. It was an old haunt of the writer and antiquarian, Horace Walpole. This was first established near Baldwin's Bridge (first mentioned in 1274) over a backwater of the Thames in 1511. However, it gained such a terrible reputation that the Provost at the College had it closed down, and it later reopened in the present building which had previously been a magistrates' court. The former Cockpit Inn dates back to 1465. It was once a pub known as the Adam and Eve but changed its name because the knucklebone flooring (that survives) at the rear of the building was mistakenly thought to have been the scene of many cock fights. It was actually an abattoir. King George III is said to have enjoyed a tipple at the old Sun Inn in the High Street.

Eton has a second northern river crossing over the Chalvey Brook at Beggars' Bridge (aka Eton Bridge aka Spital Bridge). This was first put up by Walter le Teb in 1252. The road between the two crossings suffered constantly from the heavy traffic into Windsor. In 1537, the College was obliged to have labourers working on it for three days in preparation for Queen Jane Seymour's funeral. The funerary procession from London was met at Eton by the Bishops of Lincoln and Carlisle, while poor men, wearing the Queen's badge and holding torches, lined the High Street. In 1727, the Slough Road which leads up to the main Bath Road, became part of the Colnbrook Turnpike toll road and conditions there were considerably improved.

These easily accessible roads led to the King keeping his horses in Eton. A royal stable was located on the site of King Stable Street sometime before 1511 and was still there in the 1750s. This may have been why King Richard II's uncles, the Dukes of York and Gloucester, met with representatives of the London mayor at Eton in 1392. They were enquiring into the management of the City as the citizens had refused to lend the King a requested thousand pounds.

Back in 1440, the famous college – officially the 'King's College of Our Lady of Eton beside Windsor' – had been founded by the pious King Henry VI and in the following reign it acquired Eton manor. The King provided the College with numerous endowments so that it could provide free education for 70 poor boys in preparation for attending King's College, Cambridge. However, during the Wars of the Roses, Henry's rival, King Edward IV, transferred most of these assets to St George's College at Windsor Castle. Construction of Eton Chapel and its cloisters had to be halted. The former never did reach its planned eighteen bays – it currently has eight – though it does contain a spectacular series of Flemish wall paintings produced from 1479–87 but lost for 300 years after 1560. For a short period after the foundation, it was a great pilgrimage centre with the unusual right to grant indulgences reducing punishments in purgatory.

Figure 51: Queen Jane Seymour's funeral approaches Eton

The College, including the great tower gate, was eventually completed by Provost Roger Lupton in 1517. Life was spartan for both boarding pupils and, increasingly, for others living in 'houses' in the town (which were formalized from 1722). The boys rose at 6am for their lessons, which were entirely in Latin, and finished at 8pm, with only an hour's break during the day.

There were only two three-week holidays and one of those was spent at College. In the 18th century, Eton College particularly flourished under the patronage of King George III, who visited the boys often. Later, from 1861, the accommodation, curriculum and staff were all improved following a report from a general boarding school investigative commission. By 1891, there were over 1,000 boys at the school, just slightly below the current figure. The traditional uniform of black tailcoat, waistcoat, false-collar and pinstriped trousers was formalized around this time. Over the years, pupils have included many well-known scholars, writers, artists, scientists, soldiers, churchmen and statesmen, including 20 British Prime Ministers, but perhaps the most famous 'old boys' have been fictional, such as James Bond and Captain Hook.

The village had had its own chapel on the site of the current college graveyard. In the early 13th century, Baron Cantilupe from Hambleden, the father of St Thomas Cantilupe, gave its advowson (the right to appoint the priest) to Merton Priory, who were big landowners in Upton, in return for the right to erect his own private chapel. By 1487, the village chapel had fallen into ruin and was pulled down. The parishioners took to using the College Chapel instead, until a chapel-of-ease was built on the present site in the High Street in 1769 and rebuilt on a larger scale in 1819. Bizarrely, the congregation faced the altar in the west. The box for the parish watchman (an early type of policeman) is known to have stood against its east wall. The present church was built in 1852. It had a spire that was removed a hundred years later. In 1981, falling numbers led to its closure and it has since been converted to the College Sanatorium and local medical centre with a small chapel on the upper floor of the old chancel.

Growth of the High Street was constrained by the River, the College and the Great Common which retained the rights for commoners when other local parishes were enclosed in the early 19th century. Slightly to the west, the name Eton Wick indicates a dairy farm – on the site of the present 18th century Manor Farm – attached to Eton manor on the edge of the parish. Other local old farmhouses include Bell Farm dating back to 1375. This area was ideal for development during the 19th century, although the majority of the western portion of Eton Wick was historically over the border in the old parish of Burnham. Its church was built in 1866-67. Both areas became part of Berkshire in 1974.

The Fisheries

Figure 52: West Court, home of architect, William West Neve

This is the south-eastern tip of Maidenhead, spilling out towards Bray. Originally this was one of the areas of common grazing land for Bray parish and was called Oldfield. Archery meets were held there in Elizabethan times, as commemorated on an ancient brass plate in Clewer Church. The Maidenhead and Bray Cricket Club dates back to the 1750s and Oldfield was one of its first cricket grounds.

Mrs Annie Smith was the first person to build a country house called The Fishery near the railway, in 1870. The name came from one of the four lucrative fisheries for which Bray was to be justifiably proud in medieval and later times: the Maidenhead Bridge Fishery. This was a hive of activity for the fishing and associated industries. There were numerous fishing weirs and osier beds made up of willow trees for making the wickerwork traps. The industry only began to decline with the introduction of river pollutants in the late 18th century. Ironically, Mrs Smith had to sell up after an unsuccessful court action over fishing rights on the Thames. The area was developed for housing from 1890 and boasts some superb late Victorian riverside villas of timber-framed Arts-and-Crafts style.

Bray Lodge, now split into four houses of varying names, was reputedly erected for Lily Langtry, the mistress of King Edward VII. They enjoyed Maidenhead society and often ate at Skindles on the Taplow bank of the Thames. Oldfield was built as the Guards Club, providing leisure facilities for the Grenadier Guards officers stationed at Windsor Castle. It eventually became the home of the art collector, Henry Reitlinger. After his death in 1950, his daughter transferred her father's collection there from the Museum of Fine Arts in Bern (Switzerland) to create the Reitlinger Museum. This closed in 1987. The collection is now part of the FitzWilliam Museum, Cambridge and the house is the River Arts Hotel. West Court was designed by the architect, William West Neve, as his own home and completed in 1899. Like Oldfield, it has a romantic turret taking full advantage of its riverside views. Neve lived there for 43 years, ran the Maidenhead Regatta and was noted for his local philanthropy.

Furze Platt and Maidenhead North Town

Furze Platt means Gorse Plot where the locals collected firewood. The earliest known settlement in the area was a simple single-family Bronze Age farmstead found by excavation. Before 1876, there were only three dwellings on the Platt. Over the next twenty years, however, the area grew into a small hamlet centred around a triangle of roads and stretching south to Cordwalles College (now St Piran's Preparatory School), but still far detached from Maidenhead town. This college for sons of the London gentry, like the young Benjamin Disraeli (later Prime Minister), moved there from Blackheath in 1872. St Peter's Church was built in 1897 to replace an iron mission church.

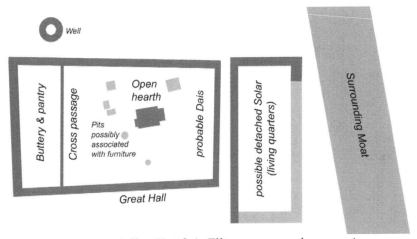

Figure 53: The Great Hall at Knight's Ellington moated manor site

Cannon Court is named after the canons of Cirencester, whose Dean owned the place at the time of the Domesday Book (1086). He was the King's Chancellor and had another house next to the church in Cookham, but the canons probably stopped at the Court when travelling between Gloucestershire and London.

Beneath the railway on Gringer Hill is Six Cross Roads, four roads of which are no longer linked. The area was originally called Craufurd Rise. At the Gringer Hill/Belmont Road Corner, where the Diamond Trading Company Research Centre now stands, stood Craufurd College, a Jewish Boarding School, that ran between 1897 and 1926.

North Town was the site of the ancient manor of Knight's Ellington, owned by the Pinkney family from Northamptonshire throughout the Middle Ages. The name is reflected in Ellington Park. The family were mostly absentee landlords renting the place to the Le Despenser family in the 1340s and 50s. Hence it is sometimes known as Spencer's Manor, with Spencer's Farm next door. The medieval manor house stood on the edge of Summerleaze Park, behind Aldebury Road. The road itself is named after the manor earthworks or 'old bury' that still survive. It was a triple moated site that was extensively excavated in the late 1960s. On the square platform in the centre once stood a Norman great hall of one large room with a divided food preparation area at one end and a hearth in the centre. There were also stables, kitchens, two wells and an industrial area.

St Luke's Church was built in 1865-6 and extended a few years later. The spire was added in 1894. Housing quickly began to grow up in the surrounding area, and along North Town Road and around the Harrow pub (now the Farmer's Boy). Dotted in between were a number of fine country houses. By the early 20th century all this had joined up with Maidenhead.

Great Hollands and Jennett's Park

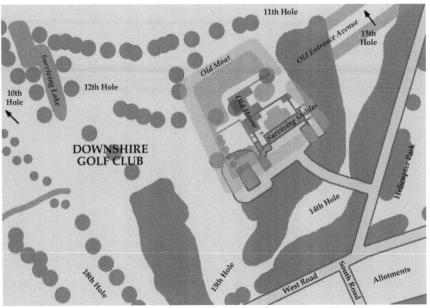

Figure 54: Plan of old Easthampstead Park's position on the golf course

Great Hollands was a medieval field-name in Easthampstead parish. There would have been a Little Hollands at one time too. They may have been named after their owner, or possibly refer to flat land. The place is now the Bracknell housing estate sandwiched between Easthampstead Park and Easthampstead Village/Wildridings. It was built in 1967 and designed so that the houses look in upon the estate and residents can walk around without the hindrance of vehicular traffic. Cars circle around the outside where the short and punchy road-names, named after London Telephone Exchanges, are arranged in alphabetical order, making an individual address easy to find. Near the shops, there is an unusual modern pub with a tree growing through the middle. Affectionately known as the Twig, it is officially the William Twig. William farmed this area in the mid-16th century and was the first tenant farmer to buy his lands from the lord of the manor. He is recorded as having been "a man of humble origin, full of initiative and not above a trick or two".

Figure 55: The old stables at Easthampstead Park

The Home Farm and Wooden Hill are slightly newer than Great Hollands. Not surprisingly, the former was built on the site of the Home Farm of Easthampstead Park. The old farm house stood where the northern side of Beedon Drive is now. It had an impressive entrance arch through the building structure which may have inspired the bridge flats now to be seen in the area. Wooden Hill is built around the site of what has usually been termed a prehistoric burial mound, between the entrances to the roads Sylvanus and Spinis. However, it has also been suggested that it may be the remains of the motte of a Norman castle. The name is certainly appropriate and dates back to at least 1800. The motte would presumably have been an early predecessor of Easthampstead Park. Legend, perhaps of no great age, makes the Park one of the homes of King Cynegils of Wessex in the 7th century. It was supposedly there that he met with King Oswald of Northumbria and was persuaded to become a Christian. Perhaps this story would be better transferred to the Wooden Hill area.

Easthampstead Park, to the west of Jennett's Park, was a royal hunting lodge built in Windsor Forest for King Edward III in 1350. It became the centre of the forest subdivision of Easthampstead Walke and was widely used by the King and his descendants: Richard II, Henry VI and Richard III who all issued decrees from the lodge. Henry VII and his son, Prince Arthur, arranged the latter's marriage to Catherine of Aragon while staying there and are said to have ridden out for their first meeting on Finchampstead Ridges. Catherine's second husband, Henry VIII, also hunted there. When their marriage turned sour, Catherine was banished to Easthampstead and other royal manors and it was there that she is said to have received her husband's commissioners. They pleaded with her to agree to having divorce proceedings heard in England but she would have none of it. Some say she was even staying at Easthampstead when she heard that the divorce had been finalized. The old moated house at Easthampstead Park stood in the middle of the area now covered by the Downshire Golf Course, just south of Easthampstead Park School and east of the lake. The cupola-adorned stables still survive.

The Park was later granted to William Trumbull on the condition that he keep up the deer park and he seems to have built a new house in 1629. A lime kiln used to make mortar for it has been excavated beneath the modern houses at Jennett's Park, as well as a small Iron Age farm with thatched round houses and granaries. Jennett's Park is named after Jennett's Hill, the small rise towards the corner of Great Hollands. This, in turn, is thought to be a corrupt form of Jenkins' Hill. Trumbull's grandson was envoy to France and Ambassador to Turkey. In his retirement, he loved to gather literary society about him at Easthampstead, including Alexander Pope and John Dryden. The present imposing Jacobean style mansion was put up on the park's northern edge for Trumbull's descendant, the 4th Marquess of Downshire, in 1860. At the time, he swept away a number of local hamlets: Cocks' Green, which stood halfway up the drive to Easthampstead Park and spoilt the dramatic approach to the new house; and Jenkins' Green (like Jenkins' Hill) which stood in the Willoughby Road area of the Southern Industrial Estate where the Marquess wanted to build his new Manor Farm.

Great Park Village

The Village sits almost at the centre of Windsor Great Park, the monarch's personal hunting ground set out to the south of Windsor Castle around 1110. Twenty-eight houses were erected for the workforce of the park in 1946 adjoining the Prince Consort's Workshops. They were designed by Sydney Tatchell and built as a model village around a triangle, in the Garden City style. Further houses were added in the 1960s. The York Club community centre, named after the present Queen's parents, was originally a Vickers Armstrong aircraft factory that was moved from near the Obelisk Pond in the Park after the Second World War.

The workshops, named upon the unexpected death of Queen Victoria's husband, Prince Albert, are typical English estate buildings largely built in the 1850s and 60s. They were designed to provide all the carpentry, sawyer, wheelwright and blacksmithing services for the Royal Estate and, remarkably, are still in use today. The trees of the Park provided all the wood for such activities over many centuries. It still has the largest collection of ancient oak trees in Western Europe. Some of them were planted over 1,300 years ago. The site of the present workshops dates from the 1830s when the Prince Regent took up more or less permanent residence at the Royal Lodge and the original ones nearby had to be found a new home.

Figure 56: The Prince Regent's cottage ornée at the Royal Lodge

The Royal Lodge is just one of a number of country houses scattered across the Great Park. They often began as small estates created, after the Civil War, when Lord Protector Cromwell sold off large sections of it. When reclaimed by the

Crown at the Restoration, the Royal Lodge became the Royal Chief Gardener's home and then that of the Deputy Ranger of the Great Park. The Prince Regent spent a small fortune turning it into the largest 'cottage ornée' ever built, complete with vast thatched roof. He then spent another fortune completely changing it all. His brother, William IV, hated the place and pulled most of it down. What was left was incorporated into a new home for the future King George VI in 1931 and the present Queen spent her earliest years growing up there. It remains the private residence of her son, the Duke of York.

Figure 57: The Copper Horse: Big enough inside for a dinner party

Cumberland Lodge was originally the Great Lodge and became the home of the Chief Ranger of the Park, a position held by many fascinating characters. Queen Anne's great friends, the Duke and Duchess of Marlborough, lived there in the early 18th century while their more famous home Blenheim Palace, which the Duchess hated, was still being built. The Duchess is most famous for keeping Queen Anne totally under her thumb until the two had a major falling out. For most of that same century,

King George II's son, the Duke of Cumberland, was in residence. He undertook a huge building programme, bred racehorses and kept an early zoo there including a cheetah which escaped. In later years, it was used by Prime Minster Stanley Baldwin to hold negotiations with King Edward VIII's private secretary over how to proceed with the crisis concerning the King's proposed marriage to Mrs Wallace Simpson. It also features in Roald Dahl's children's book, 'The BFG,' as the home given to the giant by the Queen. The core of the present house is 17th century but the Gothic revival façade only dates from 1804. It is now occupied by an educational charity.

South of the Lodge, Virginia Water was formed from a watercourse called The Windles or the Virginia River for the Duke of Cumberland in 1750. Within the angle of its two arms lies part of the moat of Old Windsor Manor House. This was made into a family home for King Edward I whose wife and children did not appreciate the uncomfortable castle at Windsor. Sadly, however, its twin great halls, chapels, private apartments and kitchens, for both King and Queen, have long gone. As a young prince, the future Edward II was banished there because of his homosexuality. When he became king, it remained a favourite retreat and he transformed one of the chapels into a collegiate church, complete with dean and chaplains. King Richard II also loved the place and had the chapel painted all over with his personal symbol, a white hart with golden antlers. The site eventually became renamed the Manor Lodge, headquarters of one of the Windsor Forest sub-divisions. Totally rebuilt in 1710, it was pulled down in 1792 and replaced, for a while, by King George IV's extraordinary Chinese-style Fishing Temple. This itself went in 1867.

There are other prominent features of the Great Park that still survive today. The 2½ mile Long Walk was planted by Charles II to rival the avenues at Versailles. The Copper Horse statue (actually made of bronze), ridden by a Roman-style King George III, at its southern end was erected on Winter Hill in 1831 shortly after 16 people had dined in its belly. Tradition says King Henry VIII had earlier waited on its site to hear the cannon fire that announced the execution of Queen Anne Boleyn. Some of the other popular features of the park such as the Obelisk, the Totem Pole and Savill and Valley Gardens are not in Berkshire but over the border in Surrey.

Hare Hatch and Kiln Green

The Hare-Hatch was one of the old gates into Windsor Forest located in Wargrave parish – presumably where hares were often seen. This part of the Forest was an area sacred to the Anglo-Saxon people and called the 'Frith' (Maidenhead Thicket is the only woodland portion remaining). The hamlet emerged on the edge of this forestland, apparently as summer pasture for local livestock, as indicated by the names of Deane Farm and the Deane fields.

Though farming always remained the main industry in Hare Hatch, the building of the Bath Road through the hamlet gave it a great boost as a stopping off place for travellers to and from London. The area was particularly well known for being frequented by highwaymen, so Hare Hatch hospitality at its six pubs was most welcome. Unfortunately, the local Hundred (like a small district council) was responsible for paying out compensation to the victims of such men and this could be subject to abuse. A particularly well-known case is recorded in

1748, when a certain Thomas Chandler claimed to have been robbed of £900 whilst travelling through the edge of Ruscombe parish – a hefty sum in those days. He somehow managed to bind his own feet and arms and hop back to Hare Hatch, where he was 'rescued' by an unsuspecting shepherd. He then reported the so-called robbery and retired to the Hare and Hounds where he dined on the story of the 'attack'. He was initially reimbursed for his losses by the Hundred of Sonning but the truth was eventually revealed and justice was served when he was tracked down living it up at a pub he had bought in Coventry.

Figure 58: 17th century Horse and Groom Pub on the Bath Road

The area north of Kiln Green is the main centre of the bear place-names of Berkshire: Bear Grove, Bear Place, Bear Hill, Bear Ash and Bear Corner. This is usually said to be where Anglo-Saxon settlers kept pigs in the fields they had carved out of the surrounding woodland. The soil was too heavy for cultivation. A 'bare' was a swine pasture. However, Bear Corner takes its name from the unusually named A'Bear family (short for Atte Bear) who lived at Hill Farm there from at least 1553 until 1895, and in the general area from at least 1318. Traditionally, they were descendants of the great Herefordshire family of De La Bere. Perhaps this family name is also reflected in the other local 'Bear' place-names.

Bear Place, where there is a fine medieval moat, may have been the original home of the A'Bears. The present house was built further east in 1784 by David Ximenes. His son, Sir Morris Ximenes, raised at his own expense and commanded the Wargrave Rangers during the Peninsular War. The family is said to have been cursed by a Catholic priest who found that this ancient Spanish clan had abandoned the old religion for Judaism and then Anglicanism. There are several other good country houses in the area, the most interesting of which is perhaps Scarletts. It was built about 1765, by James Leigh-Perrot, the maternal uncle of the authoress, Jane Austen. He lived there very happily with his wife, Jane, for many years. Having no children, his heir presumptive, James Austen, visited him there several times. It is not recorded whether his more famous sister, Jane, ever accompanied him but she did visit her uncle and aunt at their house in Bath. Poor Mrs Leigh-Perrot spent some time in prison in that unfortunate city, as well as in Ilchester, when she was falsely accused of shop-lifting.

Harmans Water and Martin's Heron

Harmans Water was developed as a suburb of eastern Bracknell in the late 1950s after the area had been designated a 'New Town' for those bombed-out of London. It was supposed to have been the final phase of building work, but other areas have joined it since. The original Harman's Water in old Winkfield parish was a large lake that stood in the middle of Sker Moor, where Merlewood and Shaftesbury Close are now. The name dates back to the 18th century or beyond, although who it was named after is unknown. Harman is not a common local name. The lake sat to the south-east of a small hamlet, below Sandy Hill, that had grown up along what's now the Bagshot Road, to the south of the 17th century Horse and Groom pub (now a restaurant) across the old border in Easthampstead parish. By the early 19th century, it had become known as Borough Green.

Figure 59: Ramslade House, the RAF Staff College, now demolished

Along Broad Lane, the area around the old Blue Lion pub was another ancient hamlet called Ramslade, as shown by two remaining 16th century cottages there. Lime kilns for making mortar, excavated just to the south, indicate that there may have been a large house on the site of old Ramslade House as early as the late 16th century. The last house was built in 1840 and in the 1890s was the home of Henry White, a prominent American diplomat working at the US Legation (consulate) in London. In 1943, the RAF Staff College moved there from Bulstrode Park near Gerrards Cross and was part of Bracknell life until the site closed in 1997. As part of the joint Defence Academy of the United Kingdom, the college then moved to the Beckett estate at Shrivenham, near Faringdon. A housing estate called The

Parks was built over the college grounds from 2004 and, despite hopes of it becoming a community centre, the house was demolished in 2016.

Ranelagh School was founded by the Earl of Ranelagh, Keeper of Cranbourne Chase, in Cranbourne in 1709. When the school moved site in the 1880s, some money was held back for the founding of a grammar school in Harmans Water in 1908. The main school block was built in an attractive Neo-Wren style.

The adjoining Martin's Heron estate was built as part of an expansion of Bracknell in the 1980s. The railway station was opened in 1988. Both were built on the parkland that once surrounded the mansion of Martin's Herne (or Heron), pulled down shortly before the development. It was originally called Goddard's Croft and was built on the edge of Whitmoor Bog, probably around 1750. The house was the residence of a succession of high-ranking army officials and minor members of the nobility. General William Gordon lived there in the late 18th century. He was Groom of the Bed-Chamber to King George III and the King was a frequent visitor to Martin's Herne. A grassy walk used to be pointed out as one that the King particularly liked to stroll along. General Gordon is best known for controlling the mob during the Gordon Riots of 1780 as recorded in Dickens' 'Barnaby Rudge'.

Holyport and Moneyrow Green

Holyport is locally thought to mean literally what it says, Holy Port, a stopping off point for pilgrims on their way from Canterbury to St David's, but old documents show that the name originally stemmed from Horrig-Port meaning Muddy

Market – thoroughly unromantic. The beautiful village green was one of several stopping places for drovers to graze their sheep in the parish of Bray. Today the place is a delightful village with lovely old buildings, including a number of pubs, set around this green. The George Inn is 16th century and retains its old brick brewhouse. The Belgian Arms is so named because, when it was previously called the Eagle, passing German prisoners of war would salute the pub sign as a symbol of their country. So the name was changed.

It is hard to believe this area was the victim of Swing Rioters protesting against agricultural mechanisation in 1830. They fired Mr Wickworth's hay-ricks, burning 10 out of 18, as well as 4 adjoining barns.

Figure 60: The Green at Holyport, with Holyport Lodge on the right

Scattered slightly further out are a number of interesting old manors and country houses. Most prominent is Holyport Lodge, the striking Queen Anne building with an Edwardian façade that dominates the green. In the mid-19th century, it was the home of George William Newell. He was a noted antiquarian, despite being both deaf and dumb. It is currently a care home. Behind is a real tennis court – one of the few left – built in 1889 for

Jewish businessman, Sam Heilbut of Holyport House. Down Langworthy Lane you will find both (John) Gay's House and Lynden Manor. The former is a much extended early 17th century house named after the man who owned the site in 1456. The latter is on another old site, but the present delightful timber framed building dates from about 1850. Before the Second World War, it was the home of Prince Philip's maternal uncle, the 2nd Marquess of Milford Haven. The Prince largely grew up there when not away at Cheam School. Slightly further east is Stroud Farm, once Stroud Hall, with an impressive array of ancient farm buildings, including a 15th century barn. The house is a partly 14th century building, dating to a time when it was called Shiplakes. At the end of that century, it was in the hands of the well-known Staverton family. William Staverton was one of the surveyors of Maidenhead Bridge but was attacked and murdered in 1401 by "certain evil-doers". Another branch of the family lived at Heathley Hall in Warfield.

Most of Holyport lies within the manor of Philberts (formerly Philibert's), which was merged with the manor Cresswells in about 1283. Both had old moated manor houses either side of the Ascot Road, just north of the green. The latter now lies under the motorway, but earthworks of the former are still traceable. It had been the home of the Lords de St Philibert, friends of Royalty. In 1345, at the age of only eighteen, the 2nd Lord and his friends went on a pilgrimage to Italy, where they were unjustly imprisoned. In retaliation, King Edward III threw all English resident Italian merchants into the Tower of London until young St Philibert was released. Unfortunately, this still took two years. Around 1550, this earlier house was replaced by a superb black and white timber-framed building. This was eventually the home of King Charles II's closest friend, William

Chiffinch, and a regular meeting place for the King and his mistress, Nell Gwynne. Sadly, this was ruthlessly demolished in 1780 and replaced by a castellated Regency Gothic revival building which, in 1860, became a military academy attended by Sir Winston Churchill. Left in a bit of a state after housing German prisoners of war during the First World War, it was pulled down in 1919. Neither of the subsequent replacements have been particularly noteworthy.

Figure 61: Philbert's Manor House, demolished in 1919

The lovely old name, Moneyrow Green, dates back to 1376. The green itself was in a triangle at the southern end of the row and this is where the first houses were built. The hamlet remained detached from Holyport until the late 20th century. Just to the south, Blackbird Lane is now not much more than a track leading to Mount Scipetts Wood Farm. However, it was once the home of the ancient Blackbird Inn, which an old ballad tells us once played host to an incognito King James I after he escaped from a very boring hunting party. Getting drunk with a local tinker, as a joke, he offered to introduce him to the King. He took him to the nearby New Lodge below Oakley Green, where he revealed his identity. The tinker thought he would be thrown in gaol, but, instead, he was knighted.

Horton

Horton became part of Berkshire in 1974. The village of Horton – meaning Vegetable Town – has always stood at the Datchet Road/Stanwell Road and Horton Road/Park Lane junction, where the attractive green survives. A mighty elm tree used to stand there and tradition tells how it was planted to commemorate the death of a child from the Crown Inn opposite who was accidentally crushed by a falling maypole on the same spot. The church, which dates back to the 13th century, was originally set slightly apart, but the village has now filled in the gap.

The old medieval manor house, with Elizabethan extensions, once stood very close to it on the south side of the church tower. It was called Place House (aka Horton Place) and was one of the homes of the Bulstrode family of Bulstrode Park, near Gerrards Cross, who were also associated with Upton-cum-Chalvey. After the marriage of Henry Bulstrode in 1602, Place House became the family's favourite residence. It was later sold, in about 1658, to Robert Scawen, an important military administrator and Chairman of the Army Committee that provided logistical and financial support for Parliament's New Model Army. His sons, Sir William and Sir Thomas, became great London city merchants and both served as Governors of the Bank of England. In the 18th century, the house was let to the Brerewood family, one of whom was a rather coarse poet who wrote about debauchery. The family laid out an extraordinary garden with a viewing mound, ornamental canals and a library built on a bridge. The feed canal remains just east of the church.

Figure 62: Old Place House at Horton, demolished in 1785

Place House was taken down in 1785 and around 1800 was replaced by Horton Manor just to the south for the Williams copper magnates from Bisham who also owned Wraysbury Mills. It had a grand copper dome. The house fell into decay in the 1970s and its site is now under the Boat Pool. Its garden canal is now part of Kingsmead Lake. The lakes were created through gravel extraction in the late 20th century and became a fishing resort from 1990. Not far away, Wraysbury Reservoir covers old Horton Common and used to be in Horton parish but is now part of Stanwell. The Queen Mother Reservoir built in 1976 is, however, half in Horton and half in Datchet.

The settlement that emerged around the Stanwell Road and Foundry Lane/Bells Lane junction was a separate hamlet called

Berkyns or, later, Mill Green. Horton (aka Colne Bridge) Mills, to the east, were important paper mills. The rags imported for the industry are thought to have brought the plague to the area in both 1626 and 1637 when its victims dominate the parish burial registers. In the mid-19th century the mills housed the thriving shawl-printing business of Messrs. Tippet and Co for some years. There was a good medieval moat just to the south-west, now built upon by the Horton Trading Estate.

Berkyn's Manor House stands just to the north. The nearby stream formed part of a large moat, two arms of which survive. John Milton, the poet, lived in an earlier house there from 1632-8. His mother is buried in the church. The place is named after the Berkyn family who were later residents. The present Neo-Elizabethan house was built by Edward Tyrrell in the mid-19th century. The last occupant, Ernest Rayner, lived there from 1945 until his death, aged 96, in 1987. The house has stood empty ever since, complete with contents, and has, unfortunately been left to rot.

Hurley

Hurley is a pretty village, down by the Thames, with reminders of its medieval monastic past scattered amongst its later houses. St Birinus is said to have inspired the building of the parish church there, around AD 700. The Vikings forded the Thames at Hurley in AD 894 when marching from Essex to Gloucester and may have destroyed this early building.

The church was rebuilt as a Benedictine priory in the mid-11th century in memory of Athelaise, the first wife of William the Conqueror's friend, Geoffrey de Mandeville, who was lord of the manor. It was dedicated by St Osmund. Geoffrey's second wife, Lasceline, had persuaded him to establish the nunnery and she was later buried there herself, along with Princess Edith, sister of King Edward the Confessor. The aisleless parish church of today is all that remains of this old Norman priory church. The 13th and 14th century refectory and other monastic buildings around the lost cloister are now a private home but can be seen through an adjoining arch. To the west is a dovecote and tithe barn. The Old Bell Inn, nearer the main Henley Road, is one of the claimants to the title of the 'oldest pub in England'. It is thought to have been the Priory's guesthouse, established in 1135. The sanctus bell hung above its door and was rung to announce the arrival of new guests. One such was Henry IV who arrived there just after murdering his predecessor, Richard II. He came to pray for the soul of his late wife but ended up discussing the monastery's privileges.

Figure 63: The Bell Inn at Hurley: the oldest pub in England?

To the east of the priory church, down by the river, stood the priory's infirmary. After the Dissolution of the Monasteries, this was converted into a mansion called Ladye Place, the home of the Lovelaces from 1545. It was named after the Virgin Mary to whom the priory had been dedicated. Richard Lovelace sailed with Sir Francis Drake and rebuilt the house in Elizabethan splendour with his share of the Spanish booty. His son was created Lord Lovelace of Hurley in 1627, and his monument can be seen in the church. The family had many connections with national events. In October 1666, the 2nd Baron is recorded to have heard a case in the Hurley Manor Court at which a certain Edward Taylor, a boy of ten, claimed that his father and uncle had started the Great Fire of London, throwing fireballs into shops and businesses. This would seem to boost the contemporary theory that it was set by Catholic conspirators. However, it is generally believed that the fire began in a baker's oven that had been accidentally left alight overnight. So, if Taylor's story was true, presumably his relatives only helped in the spread of the flames. It's not clear why the case was heard in Hurley, presumably Taylor had fled there. Other fire victims certainly ended up in nearby Windsor. Shortly afterwards, the extravagant 3rd Baron magnificently embellished the building's interior with fabulous painted rooms and ceilings by Antonio Verrio, who also worked at Windsor Castle. Later in the same century, the crypt of Ladye Place (and the old infirmary) was the scene of plotting by John, 3rd Lord Lovelace and his friends who helped bring about the Glorious Revolution of 1688 (when William III came to the Throne). The King later paid John a visit to express his thanks. The old Tudor mansion was scandalously demolished in 1837, but the crypt still survives in private hands.

The upper end of the village, on the Henley Road, is called Hurley Bottom. The old timber-framed East Arms on the corner was a pub named after the East baronets from Hall Place at Burchett's Green from the 1840s. Behind and to the west, where the houses and the football pitch are, is a natural hollow which was a popular meeting place for illegal bare-knuckle boxing matches in the Regency period. Being near the county boundary in three directions, it was easy for the organisers to escape if the authorities arrived.

Hythe End and Ankerwycke

Figure 64: King John at Ankerwycke before the Magna Carta Meeting

Hythe End means the Wharf at the End of the Parish, being located at the south-east corner of Wraysbury. One of the two mills recorded in the Domesday Survey (1086) for Wraysbury was probably Hythe End Mill on the Colne Brook. Like Wraysbury Mill, it was a paper mill in the late 19th century under Ibbotson and Ladell but, in the early 20th century, the mill closed and was converted into a factory.

The Benedictine nunnery of Ankerwycke Priory was founded in 1154 by Sir Gilbert Montfichet, the lord of Wraysbury. The nearby Ankerwycke Yew Tree was then already about 1,500 years old and may have had a religious significance in ancient times. The prefix of the name suggests that the priory started out as the hermitage of a local anchorite. It was always a very small nunnery with only about six or seven nuns, but they seem to have been a rather wild bunch over the years. There are numerous records of runaway nuns, midnight liaisons and excommunications. The last abbess was the only known nun from Buckinghamshire to have married after the Dissolution of the Monasteries. The area was only transferred to Berkshire in 1974.

When King John and the Rebel Barons met at Runnymede on 10th June 1215, King John's men camped on the Wraysbury side of the river, below Ankerwycke Priory. Five days later, the two sides sealed the Magna Carta at Runnymede. When not in the field, the King himself stayed in the sanctuary of the priory as he was concerned about possible kidnap or even assassination. At night, he would return to Windsor Castle. The nuns had to supply all parties with ale from their brewery. The young lord of the manor, Richard Montfichet, was one of the 25 barons present on 15th June when the charter was sealed. This is sometimes said to have taken place on an island in the Thames, but Runnymede itself was probably then an island, with the Thames running in a number of different channels. Magna Carta Island where the seal was reputedly put on the charter was only created in 1834 with a little Gothic memorial cottage covered in the Barons' coats-of-arms as a tourist attraction. Four days after the sealing, the Barons again reaffirmed their allegiance to the King by taking an oath, possibly beneath the Ankerwycke Yew Tree. The gathering finally dispersed on 23rd June. King Henry VIII is later said to have wooed Queen Anne Boleyn beneath the branches of the great yew.

Figure 65: 2,500-year-old Ankerwycke Yew

Today there are only a few ruinous walls left of Ankerwycke Priory. They are looked after by the National Trust. After its dissolution, the place was granted to Sir Thomas Smith in 1550 and he converted the old buildings into a sumptuous family home called Ankerwycke House. He was a well-known classical scholar and Provost of Eton who rose to be the Secretary of State. When his old friend, Doctor John Taylor, was deprived of his position as Bishop of Lincoln, he retired to Ankerwycke and died there in 1554. By the 1730s the house had fallen into disrepair and in 1805 a replacement was built by John Blagrave, a Jamaican descendant of the regicide, Daniel Blagrave of Southcote near Reading. This also eventually became derelict and was demolished in the 1970s.

Knowl Hill, Warren Row, Cockpole Green and Crazies Hill

Knowl Hill is one of those names that has two parts that mean the same thing. It straddles both the Bath Road and the parish boundary between Hurley and Wargrave. There was a Roman settlement there, including a large aisled villa at Canhurst Farm. The later community flourished on the back of the coaching trade, with inns, blacksmiths' shops and wheelwrights. There was also a brickworks for over a hundred years until 1992 and the place gained its own little brick church in 1841.

The pubs had an unsavoury reputation in times past and are said to have been frequented by highwaymen in the 17th and 18th centuries. At the Bird-in-the-Hand, one of these men was apparently celebrating, after a huge haul from a passing coach, when he accidentally fell down the stairs and was killed. On occasion, his spirit is said to still be seen around the pub.

Figure 66: The former Severn Stars, popular with highwaymen

The old Seven Stars at Knowl Hill was especially popular because it stood right on the parish boundary and criminals could escape the local authorities by simply moving from one room to another. It was outside this inn that Captain James Hind shot and killed a man. He had thought the man was chasing him after he had robbed the regicide, Colonel Thomas Harrison, of £70 on Maidenhead Thicket. Hind was an infamous highwayman of the early 1650s who only robbed roundhead supporters. In the early 19th century, Knowl Hill was famous for its illegal prize fights which could attract up to 5,000 spectators. Being on the Bath Road, the organisers could escape over the county boundary either east or west, or even north, if the authorities arrived on the scene. The boxers, who were often based at the Seven Stars, included the famous Young Dutch Sam who won his debut fight there in 1825. Unfortunately, the fighting had a tendency not to stay within the ring and often spilt out into the rough crowds looking on.

The other nearby hamlets are more rural but similar stories are told of the 17th century Dew Drop Inn, hidden away beneath Ashley Hill near Warren Row. This pub is said to have had an underground room where Dick Turpin would hide Black Bess when in need of shelter after an escapade on Maidenhead Thicket. Turpin is unlikely to have come to Berkshire, but the story could relate to some otherwise forgotten man-of-the-road. An old legend tells how Ashley Hill itself became a refuge for the Domesday Book surveyors in 1086, when they were chased away from the local manor by the owner's dogs. They carried out their survey from the top of the hill instead.

Crazies Hill, further west below Cockpole Green, may mean either Poppy or Buttercups Hill. The scent of the latter is said to induce madness but the locals say they are not crazy. The only alternative interpretation stems from a French word for Slag Heap. The hill is the site of what was once the only source of fresh water in the area. It is known today as Rebecca's Well or

Phillimore's Spring. It was restored by Reverend Phillimore in 1870 when he organised the building of its smart brick cover to a design by Gertrude Jekyll. It features Isaac's wife, Rebecca, drawing water from a well. The place's original name may have been Rebra's Well, possibly named after an early Anglo-Saxon chieftain. Close by is Summerfield House, largely built in 1790 as the town hall in the centre of nearby Henley. The façade, cupola and entrance hall were moved to Crazies Hill by a Major Willis when the new town hall was built in 1898.

Bowsey Hill, between Crazies and Knowl Hills, was named after an 18th century lady called Anne Bowsey. It was locally said to be a crossing place where dead souls congregated before being sent up to heaven or down to hell. On the night of death, you could walk up the hill and meet with the spirit of the departed. You would be able to ask them one question and they were compelled to answer truthfully, no matter what the enquiry. Bear Grove on the hill's southern slopes is usually said to refer to a swine pasture, but Bowsey's gruesome reputation may point to the Celtic word ber meaning a cemetery or possibly the Anglo-Saxon word bearo meaning Sacred Grove.

Langley and Horsemoor Green

The old Buckinghamshire parish of Langley Marish was very long and thin and stretched north to cover Middle and George Greens, Langley and Black Country Parks and Langley Corner, all areas still in that county. The wider southern portion based around Horsemoor Green and the village of Langley itself was transferred to Berkshire in 1974. The earliest known settlement in the area was a village of Bronze Age round houses on the site of Ditton Park Academy. This was later replaced by typical early Anglo-Saxon sunken-floor 'grub huts'. However, unusually, these have been radiocarbon dated to the mid-4th century when the Romans were still in power. This suggests the residents were some of the earliest Germanic settlers in Britain, perhaps hired to help protect against other European migrants.

Figure 67: The Kederminster Pew leading to the library

The name Langley refers to a long clearing in Windsor Forest. The Marish suffix comes from a late 13th century lady of the manor, Christine, Lady Monte Marisco. Her grand uncle had been Rector of Wraysbury. She was a friend of Queen Isabella and retired to Langley after the death of her husband, William, Baron Monte Marisco in 1284. Active in the settlement of Ireland, his main English lands were based around Huntspill, above Bridgwater in Somerset. He also held Lundy Island, off the Devon Coast, which he had managed to have restored to the family after his uncle had been executed for using it as a pirate base.

Langley was originally just a small hamlet around the parish church. This building dates back to the 12th century but was largely rebuilt two hundred years later. It has some wonderfully carved 'green man' heads from this latter period, used to remind the congregation to stay away from superstitious practices. In the 1610s and 20s, the whole place was refitted for Sir John Kederminster who had managed Langley Park (the manor house which is now an hotel), some way to the north, first for the King and then for himself. As well as providing the internal church fittings, he had the adjoining almshouses named after him and paid for the present church tower and a large south transept to be built. This was to house his family vault below and his family pew above. The pew is quite astonishing and one of the finest to be found anywhere in the country. Immediately next door, an old chapel was converted into a library "for the use, good instruction, better help and benefit in study of such vicars or curates as shall forever hereafter enjoy the cure or vicarage." The library interior is a magnificent work of art and an extraordinary survival. There is an ornate fireplace and walls completely lined with enclosed bookshelves, the panelled doors elaborately painted with cartouches and figures of saints and prophets and, on the inside of one set, portraits of Kederminster and his wife. The books mostly date from the early 17th century but others are older and once included the late Anglo-Saxon Kederminster Gospels, now kept in the British Library.

The manor was later purchased by Henry Seymour, a descendant of Queen Jane Seymour's brother, the Duke of Somerset. He had fought for the Royalists during the Civil War, following the Prince of Wales into exile and carrying the last message to the King before his execution. In Langley, he is remembered for having founded the second group of beautiful old almshouses near the church in 1679.

Figure 68: The Seymour Almshouses of 1679

At the junction of Langley Road, Station Road and the High Street, sits Langley Hall Primary Academy (aka Langley Place). It is a 17th century building with an 18th century façade. At one time, it was the Actors' Orphanage and Noel Coward was a director. Southwards, Horsemoor Green extends down the High Street. It was always the bigger settlement and was originally centred on the northern half, where a few older buildings may still be noted in the area of Marish Court. By the turn of the century it had extended to the southern end. Half way down, just to the east, standing amongst modern flats in Tithe Court, can be a seen a beautiful old 18th century granary, raised up on mushroom-shaped 'staddle stones' to prevent vermin eating the grain. Along with the much altered tithe barn, this is all that remains of Tithe (alias Vicarage) Farm.

The railway station at Langley was opened in 1845, although the current building dates from 1878. Housing in the area began to expand shortly afterwards. Langley Newtown (i.e. Victoria Road) just off the Uxbridge Road, between the railway and the canal, was built as a small hamlet in the 1880s. The Meadfield Estate was built at the north-east corner of Horsemoor Green from 1900. However, the main housing estates of Langley were built after the Second World War for the people of bombed out London.

In 1936, Hawker Aircraft built an aircraft factory at Parlaunt Park Farm (the farmhouse was in the Blunden Drive area). The buildings stood where the Royal Mail's Heathrow Worldwide Distribution Centre is today. Two years later, this was joined by an airfield, with grass airstrips covering most of the old farmland between Horsemoor Green and Sutton. During the Second World War, the company developed and built the Hurricane fighter aircraft there. This aeroplane played a key role in achieving victory in the Battle of Britain and, at its peak, the Langley factory was turning out a hundred a year. Before this, most employment in the area had been agricultural, although the Churchfield Brickworks was also near the railway north-east of the Church.

For Ditton Park, see Datchet

Littlewick Green and Woolley Green

The ancient name of the village of Littlewick is recorded in AD 940 as probably Hlid-Leage meaning Gate [into Windsor Forest] Clearing. The 'wick' part was added later and probably refers to a dairy farm. The houses adjoining the Bath Road are in the parish of Hurley, but the Green itself is in White Waltham.

The most famous house around this charming green is called Redroofs. It was the home of Ivor Novello, the composer and actor, "one of the most popular British entertainers of the first half of the 20th century". He purchased the house in 1927 with money from his films. He was famous for his house parties amongst theatrical society and it is said that 'We'll gather Lilacs,' from his musical 'Perchance to Dream,' was inspired by the flowers in his garden. Appropriately, the house is now part of the Redroofs School for the Performing Arts where the actress Kate Winslet was head girl in the early 1990s. The little church of St John nearby was built in 1893. It contains a 10 foot long Italian reredos painting that was found, in a filthy state, in the stables at Woolley Hall. It turned out to be a rare 15th century work showing the Adoration of the Magi.

Figure 69: Littlewick Green with Novello's [white] house on the right

The area is notorious for its ghostly visitors. The damned spirit of a headless local girl, called Dorcas Noble, is, like Herne the Hunter, condemned to lead a spectral wild hunt across Windsor Forest for resorting to witchcraft to try and regain a former lover. Whilst, a Roman white lady crosses the Green and walks through the houses. 'The White Dog of Fiennes' that howls at Fiennes Farm is thought to be a Roman hunting dog. These last two spirits may therefore be associated with the Roman villa that lies beneath the fields just south of the village. It is a fine winged corridor villa with an apsidal reception room and later additions which may indicate a number of generations of the same family lived there.

Woolley Green was the common grazing land adjoining the manor house of Woolley Fiennes at Fiennes Farm. Woolley means Wolves' Clearing [in Windsor Forest], and it was owned by the Fiennes family. There are two late 17th century barns at the farm which survive from the old manor house of the famous publishing family of Newbery from Waltham St Lawrence. Ralph Newbery, the Master of the Royal Printing House, first bought the manor house at Beenham's Heath but moved to Woolley shortly before his death in 1603. The present manor house of Woolley Hall, nearer the Green, was built about 1780 and was extended some hundred years later for George Dunn, a reclusive bachelor and amateur astronomer who built himself his own observatory in the grounds. In the early 20th century, it was the home of Walter Cottingham, the Canadian paint magnate. It is now apartments.

Maidenhead

The 16th century antiquary, John Leland, stated that Maidenhead was known as Alaunodunum in Roman times. His dubious source is unknown and the only evidence of Roman occupation in the town is a couple of rural villas. One on Castle Hill was extensively excavated in the 19th century, but better known is that at Cox Green uncovered on the town's southern edge in 1959.

Figure 70: The old 1726 chapel where travellers prayed

In the 9th century, the invading Vikings are said to have disembarked from their longboats at Maidenhead and fought their way through to Reading, which they subsequently made their operational base in the South of England. At this time, what is now the centre of the town was known as South Ellington (possibly the origin of Leland's erroneous Latin name), on what was soon to become the border of the parishes of Bray and Cookham. It was when this little hamlet merged with its Maiden-Hythe or New Wharf, at the nearby Thames crossing, that the name changed. The origins of the name are not necessarily that simple however. Hithe is usually accepted as Anglo-Saxon for wharf, but there are many alternative explanations available for the maiden part:

- Maegdena: Maidens' (Anglo-Saxon)
- Moed: Timber (Anglo-Saxon)
- Mawr-Din: Great Fort (Welsh Celtic)
- Mai-Eadhainn: Great Cauldron (Gaelic Celtic)
- Midden: Rubbish Dump (Norman-French)

If the name really relates to 'maidens' rather than 'new,' then these would presumably be the nuns from nearby Cookham. It is supposed that any fort or cauldron-shaped remains would have stood on Castle Hill or perhaps at Cliveden.

Figure 71: Maidenhead Bridge (1772): Site of a bridge since 1280

Castle Hill was originally known as Folly Hill, perhaps indicating the site of a tree-covered earthwork. However, it is more likely that the ruins of the Roman villa discovered there were first referred to as the 'folly' that gave the hill its name. In the 17th century, a building called Cook's Folly did stand near the Windsor Castle Inn (supposedly named after its view). This place was previously called the Fleece or Folly Inn and it is presumed that both the pub and the hill were renamed around the same time. The name was the inspiration for a later Castle Folly built through a whim of a local draper, Edwin Hewitt, in 1897 and still to be seen today. Queen Anne House, which stood at the foot of Castle Hill until its demolition in 1970, also had folly-like qualities. It was designed by Charles Cooper from the Pinkneys Green Brickworks and built, in 1880, as a showpiece for every moulding that the company made. It was later a school and then an hotel. Another folly in the town was Langton's Folly which stood on the site of the Magnet Leisure Centre. Representing the ruinous façade of a Norman church, it was built by a group of vagrants for a local brewer who wanted to obscure the view of his malthouse. Langton's Brewery was in Market Street.

In 1269, an old chapel was built at the end of Chapel Arches (aka Moor Bridge) over the York Stream (formerly Wid Brook) in Maidenhead, without ecclesiastical permission. The medieval chapel stood empty for fifty years until the Bishop of Salisbury finally allowed its use. The chapel became a stopping place for travellers praying for a safe journey and for pilgrims visiting the maiden's head after whom the town was then thought to have been named. This was said to be the skull of one of the eleven thousand virgin followers of St Ursula of Cornwall who, according to tradition, were martyred at Cologne in the 4th century. Other supposed relics of St Ursula's followers were held at St George's Chapel, Windsor. The young Maidenhead girl was long thought to have been represented on the 14th century town seal, but this is actually St John the Baptist. In reality, the town has no known connection with St Ursula, who may not even have existed. The chapel was rebuilt in 1726 but, a hundred years later, it was regarded as obstructing traffic and was torn down. Metal studs and a plaque in the pavement outside the current Bear Inn still mark where the old chapel once stood. A new church was built to the north-west.

Just to the south, on the site of the present town hall in St Ives Road – which featured as a hospital in several Carry On films – stood St Ives' Place. This hotel, historically the manor house of Ive's Manor in old Bray parish, was sadly demolished in 1957.

Further east is the famous Maidenhead Bridge. This was originally a wooden structure built in about 1280 to replace a ferry at an important crossing point of the Thames along the Saltway from Droitwich to London. It was once much longer and the parishes of Cookham, Bray and Taplow met under the central arch. There was a hermitage at the Maidenhead end and the hermit there collected offerings to maintain the crossing. In 1400, during the Epiphany Rising, the Earl of Salisbury from Bisham Abbey tried unsuccessfully to assassinate King Henry IV at Windsor and restore Richard II to the Throne. He had to flee first to Sonning and then to Reading. His followers tried to buy him some time by holding Maidenhead Bridge. They had a pitched battle with the royal forces for three days but were eventually overcome and the Earl captured and executed.

The bridge was broken down during the Civil War to limit troop movements. Fifty years later, during the Glorious Revolution of 1688, the rebuilt river crossing was almost the scene of more fighting. When the Irish soldiers of the Catholic King James II were retreating from Reading, they stopped at Maidenhead with a view to holding the bridge against the Protestant champion, William of Orange (later King William III). They set up gun emplacements and fortified a brick house in the town, but the Irishmen could not match William's Dutch army, who sent in drummers under the cover of night to sound a retreat. In the confusion, the Catholics quickly withdrew to London.

Figure 72: Maidenhead High Street circa 1900

The present bridge at Maidenhead was built in stone for Sir Robert Taylor in 1772, when tolls were introduced which continued until 1903. About the same time, Ray Lodge, a "tall stately red brick villa," was erected nearby for Sir Isaac Pocock, a British naval captain who served during the American Revolution. The house was later inherited by his nephew and grand-nephew, the Pocock marine artists, Nicholas and Isaac. Later, it was sold to the astronomer, William Lassell, who discovered moons around Neptune, Saturn and Uranus.

It was the bridge at Maidenhead that brought prosperity to medieval South Ellington and its Maidenhithe wharf. Travellers found it a convenient stopping place and inns providing accommodation soon began to appear. The earliest on record was the Bull (1459) which stood in the High Street until 1870 at the entrance to what became St Ives Road. The famous Bear first appears in 1489. The original Bear Inn stood on the site of the HSBC Bank. It was at this Bear that an early 17th century Vicar of Bray (possibly the famous singing one) refused to pay for a stranger's meal when he found he had forgotten his purse. His curate paid instead and was later made a canon of St George's Chapel, Windsor for his kindness: the stranger turned out to be King James I, who had become lost and hungry while out on a hunting party from Windsor. The Guildhall was built next door in 1777 and it once had a walkway linking it to the pub. The Bear was moved to its present site near Chapel Arches in 1845 and the Guildhall was pulled down in 1961.

Figure 73: The imprisoned Charles I reunited with his children

The Guild of St Andrew and St Mary Magdalene was set up in 1452 as an early form of local government in the town. The group consisted of about half a dozen of the local gentry (men and/or women) who could elect two wardens and had responsibility for maintaining the bridge and chapel. Because of its religious aspect, the Guild was dissolved during the Reformation, but Queen Elizabeth I granted the town a proper charter allowing for a warden, two bridgemasters and 8 burgesses in 1582. They were given a Monday market and a fair on each of the patron saints' feast days. The power to hold their own courts liberated them from the control of the manors of Bray and Cookham. New conformational charters, with slight changes, were later issued by Kings James I, Charles II and James II, the latter making the warden into a mayor.

Another well-known Maidenhead inn became the scene of an event of national importance during the Civil War. After King Charles I's capture by Parliament, he was held prisoner at Caversham Park, but was allowed a trip to Maidenhead to visit his youngest children at the Greyhound Inn. The townsfolk strew his route with flowers and Lord Fairfax, the Parliamentary commander, found the meeting so touching that he allowed the little Royals to return with their father to Caversham. This historic inn had previously been the setting for Sir Walter Raleigh's trial for treason in 1603 because the plague was rife in London. He was sent to the Tower of London but later released. The Greyhound finally burnt down in 1735 and a bank now stands on the site where a plaque records King Charles' visit.

In the 18th century, as the second stop on the popular Bath Road out of London (before Slough was fully developed), Maidenhead was one of the busiest coaching stops in the country. Ninety coaches a day passed through the town. The coaching inns were highly popular, especially at dusk, when coachmen refused to carry on over the infamous Maidenhead Thicket for fear of being held up by highwaymen. An old story tells of how the ostler at the now demolished Sun Inn used to moonlight as a man-of-the-road. He would rob the coaches on the Thicket and then comfort the distraught passengers when they arrived at the inn. The Sun could hold up to forty horses in its stables, including extra cock-horses used to pull coaches up Castle Hill. The White Hart could take fifty horses. By the 1830s, there were many horse and coach related industries thriving in the town.

The railway arrived in Maidenhead in 1838, although the first stations were at Taplow and Boyne Hill, the present station only being built in 1871. The famous brick Railway Bridge over the Thames was erected by Isambard Kingdom Brunel in 1839. It has only two arches, each spanning a vast 128 feet. The right-hand one has an amazing echo and is thus known as the 'Sounding Arch'. When built, these arches were the widest and flattest in the World and an old story tells how the Great Western Railway did not believe they would hold up. They therefore insisted that the wooden construction framework be left in place. However – in imitation of James Bedborough's work at Windsor – Brunel lowered these temporary works so that, while appearing to support the main structure, they were actually useless. Eventually, a flood washed them away, the bridge stood alone and Brunel's true genius was revealed. The bridge is the subject of the first ever impressionist painting, JMW Turner's 'Rain, Steam and Speed' (1844). The town became a popular home for commuters. Between 1801 and 1851, the population tripled and, by 1901, this number had quadrupled. The town, and especially the river, was also seen as an easily accessible fashionable resort. It became the haunt of those looking for a good time and "Are you married, or do you live in Maidenhead?" became a well-known expression. When the Brigade of Guards Club was demolished, a Victorian rubbish pit there was found to contain a large number of discarded gold wedding rings. They are thought to have been used to give an air of respectability to single ladies visiting the town with gentlemen friends.

Maidenhead Riverside

Figure 74: Edwardian pleasure seekers at Boulter's Mill Island

The Riverside area of Maidenhead was originally known as Raymead, as still reflected in the name of the main road to Cookham. The word Ray is a corruption of the Anglo-Saxon phrase Atter Eye which means At the Isle. This refers to Ray Mill Island, where a mill stood as early as the 14th century. The last mill was built in 1726 and continued to produce flour into the 1920s. It stood at the crossing of the mill stream that cuts the island in half, near Boulter's Restaurant. An old mill wheel, found during clearance work in 2011, is all that remains today but the old 17th century mill-house survives (much-changed) across the road.

Later, the name of the adjoining lock on the river, Boulter's Lock, became an alternative designation for the area. To boult means to sift flour: so the name refers to a miller. However, this was the miller of Taplow Mill, as the lock was originally built on the opposite bank of the River in the 16th century. It was moved, along with its name, to its present site in 1827-29. The lock's volume is "the largest for a masonry-walled pound lock on any English river navigation". It is most famous for featuring in the late Victorian painting 'Boulter's Lock, Sunday Afternoon' by Edward John Gregory. This clearly shows just how popular boating on the River Thames was at that period: with so many boats filled with people crowded into the tiny lock. It was especially busy on the Sunday after Ascot Week when people visited to see the rich and famous pass through on their way to Cliveden. The area boasts a number of elegant late 19th and early 20th century villas of neo-Tudor timber-framed style.

Battling Mead was a meadow down by the Thames and later a country house called Battlemead but now the site of Battlemead Close. It is said to have been the scene of a battle between the local Anglo-Saxons and a group of marauding Vikings who had landed at Maidenhead. Alternatively, or additionally, a Civil War skirmish took place there. However, the name is most likely just short for Bartholomew's Meadow.

Moss End, Jealott's Hill and Hawthorn Hill

Moss End was originally called Mosslands, an area of Warfield parish belonging to Easthampstead manor. The older settlement was Tickleback Row which is hidden away down Buckle Lane, behind the Shepherd's House pub and restaurant. The latter was originally a simple beer house and, along with the Moss End Garden and Antiques Centre, has made the place well known locally today. It was at Moss End that the inquisitive curate of Cranbourne was once found wandering in a daze after he had tried to investigate a coven of local witches. No-one ever discovered what had happened to him and an apparent conspiracy forced him to leave the area. South of Moss End and Warfield Hall once stood the now lost hamlet of Cotton Green. Only Home Farm there remains.

Figure 75: The Leathern Bottle at Jealott's Hill

Warfield Hall is best known as the home of Sir Charles Brownlow, a great benefactor to the parish of Warfield. He repaired the church tower and built the Brownlow Hall for the whole community. It used to house his library. Sir Charles had been a field marshal in the British Army, fighting in the Punjab Wars, various Indian campaigns and the 1860 China War. He inherited Warfield Hall via his wife, just after it had been totally rebuilt a little nearer to the road following a disastrous fire.

Jealott's Hill, originally Jealous Hill or Common, is the home of Syngenta's largest research and development site (formerly

Zeneca, formerly ICI). The Leathern Bottle there was the scene of a gruesome murder in the mid-19th century. Hannah Carey, the publican's wife, had been carrying on with a local man. Though her husband, John, tolerated this for some time, he eventually snapped and took to beating Hannah, both in private and in public. One particularly bad day, she had taken to her room with her bruises. John arrived home and, in a fit of rage, threw their marital bed on top of his wife and jumped up and down on her. Hannah survived, but only for a month.

The area around Hawthorn Hill is the site of a deserted medieval village, possibly wiped out by the plague in the 14th century. It was probably the place called Bras, recorded in the Domesday Book (1086), although that just indicates it was one of the two manors in Bray parish. Its proper name was Cruchfield, as still retained by Cruchfield Manor. It has been suggested that the 'cruch' part stems from a roadside boundary cross, showing where Bray became Warfield. An alternative suggestion is that it comes from Celtic Crug meaning Hill. The word may have, more specifically, referred to a burial mound, for such a barrow stands not far from the manor house. Legend says a crock of gold was dug up there after a man had a dream that ultimately led him to the burial spot. It was therefore the crock-field that really gave the settlement its name. A prominent hawthorn tree also grew on the spot: hence Hawthorn Hill.

North Ascot

Before the Tudor period, this region was just heathland known as the Black Moor (now the stream name), with an area of scrubland called Burleigh Bushes, adjoining Ascot Heath, the common grazing land for the people of Sunninghill parish. In

1553, King Edward VI and then Queen Mary Tudor paid for a new lead-lined water supply system for Windsor Castle to be laid from a spring there. The conduit stood on a site now next to Ascot Heath Library. They built a number of houses for the workers servicing the supply and the place became known as Conduit Head. Two hundred years later, King George III built the royal kennels on the edge of Ascot Heath, which did not please the locals. The curve of Burleigh Road shows where it stood.

Figure 76: Heatherdown, a school of princes and prime ministers

Development in the area, then called Burleigh, was slow and, by the mid-19th century, there were still only a few houses along School Lane and Fernbank Road. By the end of the century, the first extensions to the settlement were mostly around the (now closed) Royal Hunt pub in New Road and along the west side of Windsor Road, where a number of smart villas were built overlooking Ascot Racecourse. More development began in the 1960s until the whole area was covered in houses and is now known as North Ascot.

To the north is Thomas Sandby's mid-18th century Ascot Place, a seven-bay two-storey house with flanking pavilions and, in the gardens, the finest man-made ornamental cavernous grotto in the country. It is currently the English country home of the Emir of Abu Dhabi. To the south, Heatherdown started out as a private house, but later became a preparatory school, boasting Princes Andrew and Edward, the King of Bhutan, Prime Minister David Cameron and actor David Niven amongst its pupils. It closed in 1982 and was subsequently demolished. The Licensed Victuallers' School now occupies the site.

The Italianate Englemere House was built around 1815 for Field Marshal Lord Roberts, who had led Britain to victory in the Second Boer War. During the Second World War, it was the home of Princesses Helena Victoria and Marie Louise of Schleswig-Holstein, daughters of Princess Helena, Queen Victoria's daughter. They had grown up at Cumberland Lodge which had been their parents' residence. Englemere Pond nearby is a very ancient pool. The name's meaning, English Moor, indicates the heath landscape that once surrounded it.

Oakley Green and Fifield

As its name implies, Oakley (or Aukeley in 1220) in Bray parish means Oak-Clearing [in Windsor Forest]. When the Vikings began raiding England in the 9th century, one of their earliest battles was the Battle of 'Acleah' in AD 851, probably fought in this area (or possibly in Surrey). It was a great victory for King Aethelwulf who sent the Vikings packing. The village later grew up around some common grazing land on the packhorse and drovers' routes from Reading to Windsor. The moated site at Mills Farm was where Sheeres House stood, said at one time to have been an inn for the packhorse traders.

On the road running west from Oakley Green sits Fifield, an area of land originally covering 'Five Hides' – enough to support five families. The hamlet surrounded an important medieval manor house, Fifield Manor. It was the home of a prominent family named Norreys – although not as prominent as their very distant cousins of the same name from Ockwells at Cox Green. Sir William Norreys was an Elizabethan 'Black Rod,' a Parliamentary official best known today for leading Members of Parliament to hear the Queen's Speech at the Opening of Parliament. He has an unusual incised marble monument in Bray Church. The old house at Fifield no longer stands, but its moat remains as an L-shaped pond.

Figure 77: The gates to Braywood House at Oakley Green

The area contains a number of other reputed manor houses, notably Bishop's and Kimber's Farms. By far the most impressive is New Lodge. This was built in 1857 for Jean-Sylvain Van de Weyer, the Belgian Minister to the English Court. Until recently it was the home of a technical publishing company but is being turned into a private house once more. It is in the neo-Jacobean style and was then the centre of the large Braywood Estate, complete with a (now demolished) estate church. The founder's tomb can still be seen in the old churchyard next to Braywood House which was previously the vicarage. The house replaced an earlier version of unknown date. The Duke of Cumberland is thought to have lived there when he was first appointed Ranger of Windsor Forest. In the 15th century, it had connections with the nearby royal kennels and was the centre of New Lodge Walke, one of the sixteen sub-divisions of Windsor Forest. It was probably the 'newest' of these royal hunting lodges, and was unusual in having fallow, rather than red, deer to hunt. An old ballad tells us it was there that King James I brought an unsuspecting tinker he had met near Moneyrow Green and knighted him.

Old Windsor

There was an Anglo-Saxon royal palace in Old Windsor, the predecessor of Windsor Castle. It is mentioned in several charters of King Edward the Confessor's reign. In 1061, the new Abbot of St Augustine's Abbey in Canterbury was appointed there and consecrated in the parish church. Legends also tell of several other events. The saintly King is said to have cured the blind there. Earl Godwin of Wessex apparently choked to death while dining with the King at Old Windsor (or Winchester). He proclaimed that he should be struck down if he was lying when he claimed not to have murdered the King's brother. He promptly dropped down dead. His sons, Tostig and Harold (later King Harold II), are said to have fought there in the King's presence and pulled each other's hair. They were probably children at the time.

The palace stood near the church in the field known as Kingsbury, i.e. Kings Borough. Part of this area was excavated in the 1950s. The complex appears to have started out as a very small settlement around AD 600. It expanded slowly during the 7th and 8th centuries, until a vast transformation took place around the year AD 800. It may have become the home of King Egbert of Wessex, who annexed most of Southern England around this time. For this was when the Royals took to building their elaborate residential complex, perhaps even more splendid than the one excavated at Cheddar in Somerset. There was a triple-wheeled watermill on an artificial millstream nearly a mile long. Nearby was a stone building with glazed windows which were enormously expensive at this time. The complex may have been burnt down by the Vikings during raids around AD 900, but it was soon rebuilt with heavy timber-framed buildings. Finds range from domestic cooking pots to a gilt-bronze sword-guard.

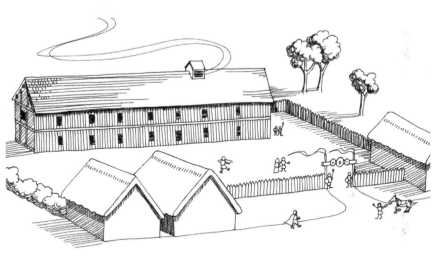

Figure 78: An Anglo-Saxon Palace

Just west of the village are three interesting old moated sites. The origins of the one on St Peter's Hill are, as yet, unidentified and little of it remains. Just to the north, however, three good arms of a moat survive surrounding Tileplace Farm, at the end of Clayhall Lane. This is the old manor house of Tile. The family who lived there, from at least 1170 to 1580, took their name from the place. Thomas Tile was Chief Butler to King Richard II and Constable of Windsor Castle where he died in 1390. He and his father had (now lost) brasses in the parish church but his initials can still be seen in the window opposite his old tomb.

Figure 79: The bizarrely named old Bells of Ouseley at Old Windsor

The third moat is the best preserved but hidden in the woods, at Bear's Rails just to the south-west. An enclosure there was once used as a home for unfortunate bears used in royal bear-baiting events. It lies just within the pale of Windsor Great Park and earlier was the site of the manor house of Wychemere. This was one of the places given by King Edward II to his friend, Oliver de Bordeaux, a slightly earlier Constable of Windsor Castle. However, it was soon exchanged for other lands so that the

King could enlarge the royal park. The area within the moat was excavated in 1920. This revealed a very extensive complex of buildings around two vast halls. Oliver's Hall (erroneously believed by the excavators to have been Anglo-Saxon) was extended by the Bishop of Winchester, William of Wykeham, in the 1360s and he erected a chapel nearby. The manor house at Wychemere appears to have been pulled down by Richard II in order to make repairs to Old Windsor Manor (later called Manor Lodge). The nearby apartments called Bear's Rails Park in Crimp Hill were originally the Windsor Union Workhouse, built by James Bedborough and George Jenner for 282 inmates in 1839-40. The Gothic revival building with pretty cupola and clock had two cross wings to house men in one and women in the other. It later became part of the King Edward VII Hospital but closed in 1991.

On the other side of the road, a bit further south, is Woodside, the home of the singer-songwriter, Sir Elton John and his husband, David Furnish. The present mansion was built around 1740 for Charles, 2nd Viscount Fane (whose main house was the predecessor to Basildon Park) and gained its name a decade or so later. It was, however, largely rebuilt after a fire in the 1930s. The estate was previously called Walton's, after a late medieval owner. Other residents have included Henry VIII's great friend, Sir Anthony Browne, who stood in for him at his wedding to Anne of Cleves, and Humphrey Michel, the Elizabethan Surveyor and Clerk of Works, who stopped Windsor Castle from falling down. The adjoining estate is that of the grand porticoed Beaumont House (or Lodge), built in 1790 and turned into a well-known Roman Catholic public school in 1861. It closed in 1967 and is now an hotel and conference centre. The associated St John's Beaumont

Preparatory School, however, still continues on a nearby site just across the border in Surrey.

The nearby Bells of Ouseley has a most unusual name for a pub and is supposed to be named after the bells of Osney Abbey at Oxford. At the dissolution of this monastery in 1538, the monks are said to have tried to save the bells by placing them on a raft and punting them down the River Thames. At Old Windsor, however, their craft ran aground. The bells ended up in the oozing mud and were never recovered. Jerome K Jerome briefly mentions the inn in his 'Three Men in a Boat' (1888).

Figure 80: The old tapestry factory at Old Windsor

In the early 18th century, an unfortunate incident at Old Windsor finally led to the summoning of the Bow Street Runners to clear up the problem of an infamous band of local robbers. They were known as the Wokingham Blacks because of their camouflaged faces. A member called Hughes had been fined £10 (approximately equivalent to £1,000 today) and had had his guns confiscated by a Keeper Miles of Old Windsor. The Blacks arrived in the night and threatened to burn down the keeper's house. When his son tried to mediate, he had his head blown off. The keeper only escaped when the next lot of powder flashed in the pan. The gang then fled but later descended on the churchwarden's house where, rather than have his home burnt to the ground, he was obliged to return the £10 fine.

Later in the same century, Old Windsor became the home of one of the first Strawberry Hill Gothic buildings in the country. The connoisseur and collector, Richard Bateman, brother of Viscount Bateman and friend of the writer and antiquarian, Horace Walpole, took a liking to a local inn in 1730. First he orientalized the building, then in the 1750s turned it into a mock monastery called The Priory, complete with cloisters and the tomb of a 13th century Welsh bishop brought from Herefordshire. It was later the home of King George III's daughter, Princess Elizabeth.

In the 1870s and 1880s, Old Windsor became well known for its tapestry industry and French weavers almost took over the village. They made up about 100 families in a population of only just over 1000. The Old Windsor Tapestry Manufactory had been founded in 1876, by Prince Leopold, as part of the Arts-and-Crafts Movement then sweeping the Country. The weavers were brought in from Aubusson in France and worked on 'low-warp' looms on which tapestries were woven on the reverse. They could only see the frontal design using mirrors. They produced superb tapestries, including sets of the 'Merry Wives of Windsor' and the 'Tales of King Arthur'. They won prizes over and above the French at the Paris Exhibition of 1878 and patrons, of course, included the Royal family. However, fears of a large industrial development being established so close to Windsor Castle led to the manufactory's closure in

1890. The beautiful weavers' hall which was retained as a village hall for many years is now a series of flats called The Tapestries.

Owlsmoor and College Town

These two suburbs cover the eastern side of Sandhurst parish. The name Owlsmoor is first recorded in 1842 but is probably much older and related to Owle Mead recorded in 1739. It was an area of the Berkshire Moors on the edge of Broad Moor Bottom, where Royalty hunted and bandits hid. The Wildmoor Heath Nature Reserve gives a good impression of this early landscape.

Figure 81: The Royal Military Academy at Sandhurst

The first settlement in the area was a small hamlet called Rackstraw's Green that grew up at the junction where the Wellington Arms stands, adjoining Rackstraw's Farm (aka Anstrum's Farm) on White Moor. The farmhouse (now a restaurant) dates back to the 16th century and was originally the old manor house of Buckhurst. Between this and the old Green is another farmhouse, that of Sandhurst Farm, built a hundred years later. This was built on the site of an old house called Cressell's which was associated with Buckhurst manor and had an estate spreading north towards Edgebarrow. The hamlet of Owlsmoor was built at the foot of Gravel Hill about 1870, not long after the founding of Wellington College nearby. Moray Avenue formed the original junction with Yorktown Road and spread up Owlsmoor Road to houses along Yeovil Road, Victoria Road/Rookwood Avenue and Cambridge Road. This area was intensively developed in the 1980s. A little iron church was built in 1880 and replaced by the present St George's on the same site in 1993.

College Town is best known today as the home of the Royal Military Academy. The RMA was established on a supposed manor estate in the east of the parish, that was purchased by the Government from William Pitt, Earl of Chatham, in 1801. Government House, the home of the commandant in the very south of the site just to the east of the Meadows Shopping Centre at Woodley Corner, is built around the old 18th century manor house. Close by are the old stables of an associated farm, originally called Lodge's Farm, where nonconformist meetings were held in the 1660s. The lake on the estate was extended out of the old millpond of Bagshot Mills on the Wish Brook. This may have been the manor of 'Hall' owned by the Atte Halle family throughout the 14th century. Its manor house may equally have stood just east of Sandhurst Church but all record of it disappears after 1498. The army moved the Junior Division of the Royal Military College to its current site, adjoining College Town, from Marlow during the Napoleonic Wars, in 1813. This was joined by the Senior Division from High Wycombe in 1858. In 1946, these were merged with the RMA from Woolwich. The main 'Old College' building, by John Sanders, is imposing but austere. The vast plain two-storeyed frontage stretches the length of the parade ground, broken only by a six-columned classical portico. This area was previously the site of an Elizabethan 'standing' or spectator stand, on what was called Queen's Standing Hill, where the ladies of the Royal Court could watch the hunting in Windsor Forest.

The settlement of College Town started with College Farm. This began life as Chislett's Farm, the home of a prominent local family of that name from at least the 1540s. Thomas Chislett was Underkeeper of Sandhurst Walke (a division of Windsor Forest) in 1586. By 1667, William Chislett, who has an heraldic ledger stone in the parish church, was Deputy Auditor of the Court of Exchequer. Expansion, of course, began after the RMC was established and its civilian employees needed homes. The first houses were in the area around where the Jolly Farmer pub has recently been demolished in Yorktown Road. This old pub was first put up in 1854 but had to be completely rebuilt nine years later as it was deemed unfit for purpose. The main area of the village, flanking College Road, was laid out on a grid system in the late 19th century.

Paley Street, Braywoodside, Touchen End and Stud Green

There are a number of small hamlets lining the Ascot Road just south of Holyport, which mostly run into one another. This is the western edge of Bray parish. Braywoodside, at the southern end, obviously indicates its position by the side of the Bray Wood. Paley Street, at the western end (actually in White Waltham parish), probably refers to a forest track through a Pagan Clearing – perhaps an open-air temple or sacred grove.

Where the roads from Paley Street and Braywoodside run into each other is a rather sharp road junction. This is Touchen End, originally Twychene (1274) deriving from the Two Chains that were stretched across each road to stop travellers and levy a toll. A less romantic translation of the name indicates it simply means Fork in the Road. Iwhurst was an alternative early name for the same area.

Figure 82: Thatched Cottage at Paley Street

Early 14th century documents show that there was once a 'Grim's Ditch' in the area. These are generally prehistoric bank and ditch features in the landscape which Anglo-Saxons found so dramatic that they thought they must have been built by the chief of their gods, Woden, also known by his nickname, Grim.

Tradition says that King George III, as Prince of Wales, made his first ever kill in front of the old Hind's Head pub at Touchen End while out stag hunting in Windsor Forest: hence the pub's name. It is now the large private house at the road junction. At the beginning of the 19th century, there were more local facilities and, in February 1800, the local bakery was the scene of a notorious local murder. Thomas Pearman, the baker, would be up early every morning baking bread for his community and would then make deliveries to outlying hamlets in the afternoon. While he was out on his rounds one day, his poor wife was attacked and beaten nearly to death with a cudgel. She died later that same evening. Two elderly customers saw a certain nineteen-year-old labourer, John Hutt, fleeing the scene. He was soon picked up by the Police and put on trial. Despite his initial denials, he was sentenced to death and hanged in Reading.

The north-eastern part of Touchen End was known as Foxley Green and this is reflected in the names of a number of the houses there. Foxley Green Farm has a superbly preserved moat, but sadly the old house was burnt down in about 1740. This was the manor house of Puckemere, another ancient Anglo-Saxon mythological name meaning Goblin's Pool. It was renamed Foxley Manor in 1321 by Sir John Foxley, a Baron of the Exchequer. He was granted licence to empark the manor and stock it with deer to hunt. His son, Thomas, was Constable of Windsor Castle; his grandson, Sir John, Constable of Southampton Castle. The latter's elaborate brass with his two wives, the first of whom he eloped with at the age of fourteen, can be seen in the parish church at Bray. In the 18th century, Foxleys, the old house at the centre of Holyport College, was the English country home of the Governor of Bengal, Henry Vansittart, although he had grown up at Shottesbrooke Park.

Shooting off at right angles from the main road is Stud Green. The name, dating from at least 1297, was originally Stert or Street Green denoting an open area of common grazing land with a forest track running through it (and heading for Cox Green). Stud Green Farm dates from about 1600 but seems to have stood alone until the following century. The hamlet was once known for its brick industry and the lakes to the north of the through road show where the clay was dug out. Sadly, the nearby Bricklayers' Arms is no more.

Pinkneys Green, Highway and Belmont

Figure 83: The Maidenhead Brick and Tile Co at Pinkneys Green

Pinkneys Green is named after the prominent medieval family of Pinkney who came from Picquigny in Northern France. They mostly lived in Northamptonshire, but also held a number of manors in Berkshire that were sometimes rented out to sub-tenants, notably Pinkney's at Cookham Dean and Knight's Ellington at Maidenhead North Town. Gilbert Pinkney was Sheriff of Berkshire in 1157 and, in Cookham Church, there was once a brass memorial to his descendant, Reverend Arnold Pinkney of Terrington in Norfolk (died 1402). Their Green was common grazing land, one of 12 local pieces in Cookham parish saved from enclosure. It had manned gates on all the roads to stop the farm animals from escaping. The area was considered largely unsuitable for agriculture and a few country houses were eventually joined, in the 1890s, by more houses built around a number of local pubs. In 1893, the Golden Ball was the scene of an unfortunate accidental shooting. Some gas-fitters from a London company were out on their annual excursion to a number of pubs in the area, when one of them found an unattended gun at the Ball. Thinking he would have a playful shooting match, he picked it up: but the gun went off without warning and he shot both his best friend and a local Pinkneys man in the head.

Figure 84: Highwaymen frequented Maidenhead Thicket

A more remote residence, which stood until around this same time, was Belmont House at the corner of what are now Belmont Crescent and Belmont Road. The Cookham Union Workhouse was housed in an old country house in North Town until 1834, when it had new premises built which are now incorporated into St Mark's Hospital in St Mark's Road. The associated church was built in 1873. The name of the complex changed from the Cookham Union to the Maidenhead Union Workhouse in 1896 when a new Guardians' Boardroom was added with a fine terracotta pediment.

The major medieval industry on the Green was pottery making. It lasted from the early 13th to the 15th centuriy. Some eleven pottery kilns have been excavated in the Camley Gardens area. The Green is rich in 'brickearth' and brick and tile production may have begun there in Elizabethan times. In 1825, the Cooper family founded a major brickworks, famous for its terracotta mouldings and gargoyles. It was later called the Maidenhead Brick and Tile Company and lasted until 1968.

This western side of Maidenhead was a favourite spot for highwaymen who preyed on travellers moving between Reading and Maidenhead. The junction of the A308 with the Cookham Dean Road is known as Hangman's Corner. It was originally the site of a local gallows or gibbet where such men of the road were hanged. It is said that, even today, horses refuse to pass by this gruesome spot. The Maidenhead suburb of Highway is named after the farm that once stood in what is now Highway Avenue. Next door was Aunt Turpin's Cottage with an unlikely reputation as a place regularly visited by her famous nephew, Dick Turpin, the highwayman from Essex. A similar but more elaborate story is also told of a house in Sonning, so perhaps she moved about a bit. The tollhouse and gate for the Maidenhead Turnpike Road, created in 1718, stood not far away near the Tollgate cul-de-sac.

However, it was Maidenhead Thicket in particular which for centuries had the unsavoury reputation for being a wild, lonely and dangerous place frequented by footpads and bandits. It was once part of Windsor Forest, stretching for five miles and covering a much greater area than the little piece of National Trust woodland that is left today. Troops camped there on several occasions during the Civil War. In Elizabethan times, the Vicar of Hurley was even said to have been paid danger money for having to cross the Thicket to preach in the chapel at Maidenhead. Unfortunately, he was usually relieved of his earnings on his return journey. In later years, the Thicket was certainly a favourite spot for highwaymen and it was there, in 1650, that the infamous Captain Hind robbed and berated Colonel Thomas Harrison, the regicide and leader of the 'Fifth Monarchist' sect, for his extreme Puritan and Parliamentarian views. It is also sometimes claimed that the Thicket was the location of Claude Duval's famous hold-up in which he only took a quarter of the £400 available in return for a dance with the lady of the coach. However, Bagshot Heath at Swinley and Hounslow Heath may have stronger claims.

The Thicket used to be called the 'Frith' (as reflected in the name of Bigfrith in Cookham Dean). This is an Anglo-Saxon word meaning Safe Place or Asylum, hence its appeal to the criminal fraternity. Did they hide there even way back then? Friths were deemed untouchable sacred places and, on the Thicket, there are several ancient earthworks. The most prominent is Robin Hood's Arbour. Excavation has shown that this banked enclosure was occupied from the Iron Age into the early Roman period. Its exact nature is uncertain, but the excavators suggested a simple farmstead. It could, however, have been an Iron Age sacred grove. Robin Hood has been interpreted as Celtic Rhi-Ben-Hydd meaning '[Place of] the King with the Head of a Deer' i.e. the Celtic horned God of the Countryside, Cernunnos. At the very least, Robin may represent the Spirit of the Woods or Green Man after whom many a pub has been named. He too has his origins in Cernunnos.

Figure 85: Cernunnos, Celtic God of the Countryside

All these places remained small hamlets until the 1890s, when house building moved them closer to Maidenhead using the bricks from Cooper's Brickyard. In 1910, the 1st Pinkneys Green Guides registered as the first company of girl guides in the country, under the patronage of Agnes Baden-Powell. She had been asked to set up the organisation by her brother after he was approached at a Scout rally by a ticketless group of girls from Pinkneys Green hoping to join in. They still meet at their original home, the Scout Hall in Winter Hill Road.

Poyle

Poyle sits at the western end of the northern runway of Heathrow Airport. Historically, it was part of the parish of

Stanwell in Middlesex. It was transferred to Surrey in 1965 and thirty years later was joined to Colnbrook as a new parish in Berkshire.

Poyle House stood between the Bath Road and Poyle Road. The Hilton Hotel at London Heathrow Airport Terminal 5 was built in the park immediately east of the site in 2000. The manor house of Poyle had stood there since the early 11th century and is probably one of the sub-estates of Stanwell mentioned in the Domesday Book (1086). It was then a timber hall owned by the Poyle family. In 1265, they seem to have become embroiled in the Barons' War. The estate was plundered by the men of William Beauchamp and John Purden, presumably forces on the opposing side.

By the early 16th century the manor was owned by the Crown. The house was rebuilt in brick and leased out to some interesting characters who may have spent a little time there. Nicholas Hilliard, the famous painter of miniature portraits held it from 1587 to 1591 and then Thomas Ridley, grandson of Bishop Ridley's cousin, from 1591 to 1629. Thomas Ridley was well known in ecclesiastical circles himself, being Chancellor to the diocese of Winchester and Vicar-General to the Archbishop of Canterbury as well as Provost of Eton.

By the time the old Georgian house was built, around 1700, the place had lost its manor status. It was probably remodelled by Sir Francis Leigh (died 1711), sometime Mayor of St Albans, but his main estates were in Hertfordshire and Kent. Over time, despite its Palladian pretentions of grandeur, Poyle House became more of a simple farm. The 19th century country house was the home of the well-known obstetric physician, Alfred

Meadows. He wrote the Manual of Midwifery (1870) which was a core medical work of the time. The house was, unfortunately, gutted by fire in 1969 and was subsequently demolished.

Poyle was on the main Bath Road west out of London but, unlike Colnbrook, never developed as a travellers' rest. However, when the Colnbrook Turnpike Trust was established in 1727 to improve the road as far as Maidenhead, the eastern toll house was set up at the junction with Poyle Road, collecting tolls from Londoners for the next 150 years.

Figure 86: Poyle House, built in 1700 and gutted by fire in 1969

Poyle Mill was associated with the manor as early as 1299. It stood on the Wraysbury River, roughly on the site of Windsor House in Riverside Park. By 1636, Richard West was running it as a paper mill, like several others in the local area. In the mid-18th century, Henry Bullock expanded this to leatherworking, but it returned to paper under Ibbotson and Sons in the late Victorian era. It had ceased operations by 1956.

Shortly before the First World War, an explosives factory was established at Poyle. It was later given its own railway station, now long gone. Other factories joined it in the 1930s and by 1956 there were over 70 more. There are now six industrial estates, mostly serving Heathrow Airport. Perhaps the most famous company to find its home in Poyle was the Formula 1 McLaren racing team in 1965. During McLaren's time there, their driver James Hunt won the 1976 championship over Ferrari's Nicki Lauda. Their rivalry made frequent headlines and was made into a film, 'Rush,' in 2013.

Priestwood and Temple Park

Priestwood Common was originally common grazing land adjoining the Chavey Down area. In times past, it was popular with highwaymen. The area historically stood in Warfield parish and appears to have been named after the monks (not priests) of Hurley Priory, who were lords of the manor there in medieval times. Since the post-war housing estate was built, there have been various reports of ghostly monks in the area.

The common land was 'enclosed' and parcelled out to individual owners in 1817 and 1827. By the mid-19th century, a small number of villas of the gentry had been built along the Wokingham Road: Priestwood House, Brook House, Oxford Villa and Ramstead House on Rounds Hill, along with the Bridge House pub. A colourful character called 'Jubilee Plunger' used to rent Brook House (opposite the pub) in the early 1890s and throw exotic parties there during Ascot Week. One of the regular guests was reputedly Oscar Wilde, who later used the name of the adjoining town for the character of Lady Bracknell in his play, 'The Importance of being Earnest'. The last remaining villa, Priestwood Court, was built slightly later than the others, around 1890, on the site of an old gravel pit. Initially the home of the Gilder family, it was converted into the Admiral Cunningham Hotel in 1954 and opened by the admiral himself.

The Garths from Haines Hill in Hurst were another well-known local family who have left their mark on the area. Thomas Colleton Garth was the master of Bracknell's local fox hunt from 1855 to 1902. The hunt, which dates from the late 18th century, was eventually named after him. The kennels were in Kennel Lane from 1919 to 1962. Today the Garth Hunt is part of the Kimblewick Hunt based in Aylesbury, but Garth Hill School in Bracknell still bears the family name.

Figure 87: The Admiral Cunningham at Priestwood

Other early buildings in the area were a handful of cottages near a Primitive Methodist Chapel in what is now the northern end of Downshire Way. In the 1890s, the triangle to the east was developed and joined to the Skimped Hill area at the end of Bracknell High Street. Later, the first houses of Bracknell New Town were built in Priestwood in 1951.

Temple Park is over the border in Binfield parish. It was built on fields between Park and Manor Farms, where there were originally only four small labourers' cottages: two where the end of Hitherhooks Hill now stands and two on the site of the tennis courts at the Jock's Lane Recreation Ground. The two woods that survive today were original features called Tinker's and Jock's Copse. Jock's Lane (anciently Tippett's Lane), along the southern edge of the estate, and the wood were presumably both owned by a local character of that name. The lane has a reputation for being haunted, but by whom, or what, is unclear. The Binfield Road, travelling on Frampton's Bridge over the Cut (originally the How Brook) joins Jock's Lane up to Temple Way. This latter road was an old lane that turned south-east from the Binfield Manor estate to complete a triangle but it disappeared around 1800. However, it survived as a field boundary and was re-instated when the Temple Park estate was built in the 1990s.

Remenham and Aston

Remenham means Ravens' Home, possibly because it was an area sacred to the chief Anglo-Saxon god, Woden, whose symbol was the raven. The village has been very small since most of the population was wiped out by plague in 1664. It is most famous for its associations with rowing and, since 1839, especially with the Henley Royal Regatta and the Leander and Remenham Clubs. It sits on the Berkshire side of the Thames just across from Henley and provides accommodation for spectators, judges and marshals during Regatta Week. The start of the course is at the Greek-style temple on Temple Island in Remenham. It was designed by James Wyatt in 1771 as a folly for Fawley Court, on the Henley side of the river.

The old manor house stood near Remenham Farm, where parts of the moat remain. From the 1160s, it was the Thames Valley home of the De Montfort family from Beaudesert Castle and Coleshill Hall in Warwickshire. It was probably from Remenham that Robert de Montfort set out for Reading to fight and win a renowned trial by combat on an island in the Thames. The manor was given a deer park based on Remenham Wood by Peter de Montfort in 1248 and was later the refuge of Sir Edmund Montfort during the reigns of Kings Edward IV and Richard III. He had been a prominent Lancastrian during the Wars of the Roses and had been a good friend of Edward's rival, King Henry VI, and therefore had all his manors except Remenham confiscated in 1474.

Figure 88: Temple Island, where the Henley Regatta races start

The parish has a number of other fine country houses. Remenham Place was a preparatory school at the beginning of the 20th century and pupils included the ill-fated Antarctic explorer, Captain Oates. Culham Court (originally in Wargrave parish) stands along the Thames path just east of Aston. It has a delightful deer park with a public footpath right across it. The old house having been burnt down during repair work, the present house was built in 1770-1 for Richard Michell, a London lawyer, who inherited a fortune from his father-in-law, a rich Antiguan sugar planter called William Dunbar. It was rented out to the party-loving 5th Duke of Marlborough for a while (when Marquess of Blandford) before he moved to Bill Hill in Hurst.

Michell's son-in-law often entertained the Royals at Culham as he was hoping for a peerage. For King George III, he even had hot bread brought specially by horse relay, wrapped in flannels, from his favourite bakery in London. The King knew the area well, for he grew up at the most prominent mansion in the parish, Park Place, although the present French Renaissance style building almost entirely dates from 1870. It was the chief country residence of the King's father, Frederick the Prince of Wales, during the 1740s. There are extant paintings of his children hunting in the park and it is said they liked to play under the 'King's Cedar' there.

The Henley murderess, Mary Blandy, is said to have frequently met with her lover in the park. She certainly fled to the safety of the Little Angel Inn in Remenham when pursued by the people of Henley after she had killed her father. In 1752, the year of her execution, the estate was purchased by Field-Marshal Henry Seymour Conway, a former Governor of Jersey. As a token of their appreciation for his service, the people of Jersey gave him a neolithic chambered tomb from the Mont de la Ville near St Helier. He had it re-erected at his Berkshire home as a romantic folly.

He also brought stones from the ruins of Reading Abbey to build the Ragged Arch (or Conway's Bridge) beneath the traffic lights on the Henley to Wargrave road and his Lombardy Poplars were the first to be planted in England. Conway's daughter, the sculptress Anne Seymour Damer, is associated with Henley Bridge, where she designed the masks of the Thames and the Isis. Another extraordinary folly on the Park Place estate is the former spire of St Bride's Church, Fleet Street, which stands alone in a field. It was brought there as a memorial to Queen Victoria's accession to the Throne.

Remenham's own church dates from the 13th century but was almost entirely rebuilt in 1870. The apse is a rebuilding of a Norman chancel on the site. It houses fine Siennese iron gates presented by John Noble of Park Place in 1875.

Salt Hill

Figure 89: The 'Salt Hill' Anglo-Saxon Burial Mound

Slough High Street always used to end at the Railway line. Salt Hill was a separate settlement starting approximately where the Lego offices are today and heading west as far as Tuns Lane.

The area was historically in the old parish of Farnham Royal and was apparently named after the 'Montem,' a large mound now in the grounds of the Slough Ice Arena.

Before 1847, the mound was the scene of a bizarre ceremony held every three years on Whit Tuesday in which the boys from Eton College asked travellers to "Stand and Deliver" a contribution (or 'salt') to the captain of the school. The mound itself is a 7th century Anglo-Saxon burial mound, not unlike the royal burial mound excavated at Taplow and may perhaps have once contained the remains of an ancient King of Middlesex. A short distance away, on the far side of the Chalvey Brook, is a spring known as Queen Anne's Well because that lady had had it enclosed under a stone cover featuring the royal arms (now gone). It was popularly visited for eye complaints and was probably once dedicated to St Anne and before that to Anu, the Celtic Goddess of Nature.

Farnham Mill, a water mill on the Chalvey Brook, once stood in Salt Hill Park, just east of Windmill Road. It is mentioned in the Domesday Book (1086) as having been built shortly after the Norman Conquest. Queen Elizabeth I gave it to her washerwoman, Anne Twiste, and her husband. It was later replaced by a windmill: hence the road name. Tradition says this was one of a pair called the Two Sisters, one of which was taken down and moved to Luton in Kent before it burnt down in 1887.

Like Slough, Salt Hill was a major stopping point for travellers on the Bath Road. Legend says that one of those who was happy to rob them on the road was a highwayman called Ledger who was eventually caught, hanged and gibbeted at the junction of the Bath Road and Ledger's Road. The area featured many well-known coaching inns but only the 18th century Three Tuns survives. The Windmill Hotel was an inn of similar age, just south of the old mill, with extensive 'pleasure grounds' across the road (where the Reckitt Benckiser building is). It was usually called Botham's after successive owners from that family: Thomas Botham (died 1837) and his son, William Hallam (died 1877). The place was popular with politicians and Royalty and the Prince Regent held a breakfast there for the Emperor of Russia, the King of Prussia, the Prince of Orange and others in 1814. Four years earlier, the American artist, Washington Allston, was taken ill there for several days and his friend, the poet Samuel Taylor Coleridge, came to look after him. The place burnt down in 1882. A smaller replacement stood on the site of the current Windmill Care Home. Watercress grown at the back of the inn was well known in the London markets in the early 20th century.

Figure 90: The Windmill Hotel where princes and politicians stayed

The Castle Inn was named after its fine views of Windsor Castle. It also had beautiful gardens (now Glenworth Place) but was rather expensive. One innkeeper called Partridge was advised to "change his name to Woodcock — on account of the length of his bill". It was during the time of this licensee that, on 28th March 1773, the commissioners of the Colnbrook Turnpike met for one of their regular dinners at this inn. Reports vary but there seem to have been eleven in the party, ten of whom were immediately taken ill and eight of whom died very soon afterwards. At the time, the deaths were a great mystery and, after much discussion in the papers, it was assumed the party had caught some infection from a number of paupers they had interviewed before dinner. The man who did not fall ill was walking in the garden at the time. However, years later, on her deathbed, Mrs Partridge blamed the incident on a cook who had been brought down from London especially to prepare the turtle soup. The turtle had been covered in its dressing the night before and later cooked in the same copper pan. The acid dressing had reacted with verdigris in the bottom of the pan and poisoned the commissioners. The inn survived the incident but eventually closed in 1841. Though much reduced in size, part of the building survived until 1964.

Sandhurst

Ambarrow is the western side of Sandhurst parish, but it could hardly be called a hamlet. Ambarrow and Edgebarrow Hills are said to be the result of some great battle between the Anglo-Saxons and the Vikings, the dead from each side being buried beneath them. In fact, both are perfectly natural hillocks. The grounds of Ambarrow Court are now an attractive country park, especially when the bluebells are in bloom. The huge old house there was built for Lieutenant-Colonel George Sheppard Harvey in 1885. It was his retirement home after having served his country in the Royal Artillery, particularly in China. The Royal

Aircraft Establishment moved in during the Second World War but the place was demolished in 1969.

Figure 91: Rose and Crown alongside Giles' Blacksmith's in Sandhurst

The name Sandhurst is Anglo-Saxon and means Sandy Wooded Hill. It is built on a small eminence overlooking the River Blackwater. There was a royal hunting lodge there at the centre of Sandhurst Walke, an important sub-division of Windsor Forest. Hart's Leap Road is thought, by some, to be the site and marks the very edge of the Forest. King George III is said to have been its last royal visitor. He used to like hunting in the area but, one day, got drenched while chasing a deer in Mill Lane. He managed to cross the River Blackwater to Yateley Mill, but, not recognising him, the miller nearly did not let him in. Luckily, his wife was more welcoming and the King returned to Sandhurst in her husband's dry clothes. Centuries earlier, Prince Arthur, elder brother of Henry VIII, crossed the Blackwater, at the same spot on his way to meet his future bride, Princess Catherine of Aragon, at Dogmersfield Park near Fleet in Hampshire.

In Georgian times and before, Sandhurst was a dispersed settlement, although the main village was centred around the area of the Rose and Crown and Duke's Head pubs. This had spread out from the area around the church onto what was then called Perry Moor, a name still represented at Perry Bridge. A number of Victorian villas then joined the landscape, though few survive. Hart's Leap is a beautiful Arts-and-Crafts house, complete with a belvedere tower, that was built for Mrs Harriette Blakely in 1875-7. The pretty well on Scotland Hill (alias Long Down) is a memorial to her mother. Harriette had previously lived at nearby Forest End which she built in 1869 after the death in Peru of her husband, Captain Theophilus Alexander Blakely. He had founded the Blakely Ordnance Co in 1863 and invented the Blakely Rifle that was particularly popular with the Confederate Army during the American Civil War. It features on his memorial in the churchyard.

The manor house of Sandhurst is in the Ambarrow area. It is called Sandhurst Lodge and stands on the edge of the parish some way from the usual position adjoining the church. It may contain remnants of a late 18th century house built by and for Richard Heaviside, the associate of the architect, John Nash. However, the place was almost entirely rebuilt for Robert Gibson in 1858, in a rather unexceptional Italianate style. It was later the country home of the well-known London solicitor, Sir William Farrer. He married one of the Shaw-Lefevres from Heckfield, over the border in Hampshire, and the couple laid out a famous garden in the grounds with large heated ponds of exotic water-lilies. They took a great interest in village life and are commemorated by a fine Greek revival monument in the parish church.

The Church of St Michael and All Angels was originally a chapel-of-ease to the mother church at Sonning. The present building, with its Surrey-style spire, dates almost entirely from a rebuilding of 1853. The main doorway is imitation Norman but may be a replica of one in the old church. The font is a remarkable object carved by the rector's daughter, Jane Monkton Jones, and inspired by the beautiful Norman fonts of Herefordshire. There are a few interesting old relics inside too, including an ancient brass to Richard Geale and his wife (1608).

Figure 92: The Neo-Norman Font in St. Michael's Church

The Geales were a prominent Sandhurst and Yateley family. In the mid-18th century, they owned the Rose and Crown, the oldest of the seven surviving pubs in the village. In the 1850s, two of the pubs were still run by members of what was by then the Giles family, local farmers who apparently liked to retire into licensed trade. However, one George Giles was arrested in 1858 after he got drunk at the Wellington Arms in Sandhurst and, apparently unprovoked, stabbed his friend outside in the road. The victim only survived because Giles hit his rib. There are two pubs named after the Duke of Wellington in the village and there is another in Crowthorne (there were once a total of three in Crowthorne). Crowthorne was part of the parish of Sandhurst until 1874 and the Duke's greatest memorial, Wellington College, was built there in 1812. He lived not far away at Stratfield Saye House, in Hampshire, and the estate stretches into Riseley.

For Sandhurst Royal Military Academy, see Owlsmoor and College Town

Shottesbrookc

At the time of the Domesday Book, Shottesbrooke was owned by Alward, the Anglo-Saxon royal goldsmith, and it was there that the Anglo-Saxon royal regalia were forged, probably from the early 10th century. It was his skilled craft, probably undertaken at Kiln Hill on the White Waltham border, that enabled Alward to keep his lands under the Norman kings. The lake in Shottesbrooke Park is known to date from his time as a late 11th century wooden boat was excavated from its bottom. The local people produced charcoal for the gold smelting in the Great Wood and a medieval village, called Shottesbrooke Auri-Fabrorum, grew up on the Broadmoor Road, near the entrance to the park. This was probably swept away when the estate was emparked for deer in the early 16th century.

The most notable features of Shottesbrooke today are the manor house and the former Collegiate church in the park. The latter is one of the most idyllic in the county: a cruciform building, entirely of the decorated Gothic style, put up in one go in 1337 by Sir William Trussell, traditionally in thanks for beating his drink problem. He had served with King Edward III in his Scottish Wars and, having made many important and influential friends, he persuaded them all to contribute to the founding of an ecclesiastical college at Shottesbrooke. Some of their coats of arms can still be seen in the windows of the church, which is thought to have been built by masons 'borrowed' from Salisbury Cathedral. The local brazier is said to have fallen and been killed whilst placing the weathervane on the spire.

Figure 93: The unchanged medieval church and remains of the college

A college was like a monastery with priests instead of monks. Shottesbrooke was quite a small complex, with just a warden, five chaplains and two clerks to pray for the souls of the King and the Trussell family. There were more buildings for them over the wall in the area of the old farm: at least two spacious halls with parlours and high chimneys, where only a 15th century cottage survives today. These buildings were once connected to the church by a covered walkway to the little blocked-up doorway in the church's south transept.

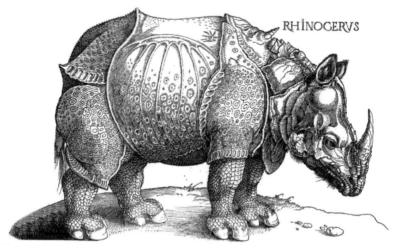

Figure 94: An Indian rhinoceros once lived in Shottesbrooke Park

Inside the church are some wonderful medieval memorials. The founder's superb decorated double monument fills the main wall of the north transept. Did it once have wooden effigies under the arches? One of the college chaplains lies in his stone coffin, and there are several fascinating memorial brasses. These include Trussell's daughter, who was one of the Pembridges from Tong Castle in Shropshire. Another, a stunning depiction of a 14th century priest and layman, has no inscription but is believed to represent a rich London fish-merchant called William Frith (died 1386) and John Bradwell, the Warden of Shottesbrooke, who may have been a relative.

The present Shottesbrooke House, next to the church, is early Tudor, extended a century later with bricks from the lake and gothicized in 1807. Its most famous resident was probably Francis Cherry, who was a pious man but a staunch Jacobite. He was therefore no great friend of the King, William III, who he saw as a usurper. The two, however, did share a great love of hunting. Cherry was a famous horseman and the King, who often met with his hounds at Shottesbrooke, became his rival. The former would risk his life at the most difficult leaps for the mere chance that the King would follow and break his neck.

Later the house was, for many generations, the home of the Vansittart family, rich Dutch merchants who made a fortune in Poland. Many members of the Vansittart family became notable members of English society. Henry Vansittart was prominent in the East India Company and a friend of Lord Clive, eventually becoming Governor of Bengal in 1759. Hoping to ingratiate himself with the young King George III who was a keen animal lover, Clive asked Vansittart to send him a number of exotic animals from India to present to the monarch. Henry packed off a Persian mare, a rhinoceros and two elephants to England. However, the captain of the ship mixed up the delivery and, instead of sending them to Clive, appeared at Shottesbrooke Park, the home of Henry's brother, Arthur, with the four creatures. What a shock Arthur must have had. Clive took offence at this misdirection, assuming Vansittart was trying to bypass him, and the two fell out with one another completely. Meanwhile, the elephants roaming in the park and the rhinoceros wallowing in the lake became quite a local spectacle, until the King came over from Windsor to collect them. The house was eventually inherited by the Smith family, who were Vansittart cousins, and they still live there today. The late Sir John Smith MP founded the Landmark Trust, a building conservation charity, at the farm next to the church.

Down the lane opposite the park entrance, you get a glimpse between the barns, of Smewyn's Manor. This moated 15th century house was supposedly favoured by Prince Arthur, elder brother of King Henry VIII, as a hunting lodge. It was later the home of the late 17th century theologian, Henry Dodwell, a great friend of Francis Cherry, who is buried in the church.

Shurlock Row and Beenham's Heath

This is the southern portion of Waltham St Lawrence parish. The name Shurlock Row is a variation of Southlake Street which was the most popular version of the place-name until the 1910s. The name dates from 1243 and refers to a situation south of Ruscombe Lake – which disappeared after the area was drained in 1820. The settlement used to spread along the Straight Mile as well as up the Street. The Shurlock area was popular with local hunts and there are records of a number of deer being killed there. One hunt that started at Shurlock Row in 1934, ended up running through the streets of Reading until the deer was finally captured in the cemetery. It is not surprising, therefore, that it was, for many years, the home of one of the several Windsor Forest pubs called the White Hart. The building dates from the 17th century and is now called the Shurlock Inn.

There are a few other interesting old buildings in the area. Great Martins is a 16th century timber framed farmhouse extended in brick a hundred years later and doubled in size in an Italianate style in the mid-19th century. The 'superior' Primitive Methodist chapel was erected in 1863 and All Saints' Church, now a private house, in 1870.

Figure 95: 17th century White Hart, now the Shurlock Inn

The ghost of a pretty sixteen-year-old is still sometimes seen waiting for her lover at the ancient river crossing of Callin's Bridge (at the top end of Callin's Lane). The unfortunate girl had found herself part of a local witches' coven before her sweetheart had shown her the error of her ways. He was a royalist soldier away fighting in the Civil War. Just before he arrived home, an angry roundhead, fleeing a small local battle, smashed up the poor girl's house and, finding her alone on the bridge, attacked and murdered her. Her spirit is thought to lead watchers to the graves of the soldiers her attacker had killed in the skirmish. The Waltham St Lawrence burial registers record another chilling death: the wife of Ralph Medwin who lived in this area, at the south-west corner of 'Ha[ ] Inneings,' on the border with Binfield parish:

1656, March 9th: Mabel Medwin, a witch about 68 years old, arraigned for witchcraft at Reading February 29th, condemned March 2nd, and executed March 5th.

Just below Callin's Bridge are the remains of an old moat, all that remains of the original Beenham's Farm. Rumour says that when part of the present 17th century house was demolished in the Victorian era, a royalist in full armour was discovered hidden within its walls. The complex retains a 16th century weatherboarded barn which may have belonged to Ralph Newbery who lived on the site. Followed by several members of his family, he travelled to London and became a famous publisher in the 16th century. His brother's descendent, John Newbery, is particularly noted for being the first proper publisher of children's books.

Nan's Oak (alias Didwell's Oak) stood near Brick Bridge, where the Drift Road crosses the Cut just east of the motorway. It was said to be the largest oak tree in the country. It was named after the Duchess of York, Lady Anne Hyde, the first wife of the later King James II. She had dined and later became ill under its branches but never recovered.

Slough

The name Slough is first recorded in 1196. It is a word mostly known today from the unfortunate expression 'slough of despond,' which stems from a fictional bog in John Bunyan's 'Pilgrim's Progress'. The local slough is thought to refer to the marshy southern portion of old Upton-cum-Chalvey parish, down by the Thames between the two villages. The name eventually became pinpointed on the river terrace at the crossroads of the London and Windsor Roads by travellers across the area. Although long distance river travel was always easier, land communications are more direct and Slough developed on one of the main medieval roads connecting London to Maidenhead, Reading and the West (now the A4). By the Tudor period, this was known as the Bristol Road. It became the Bath Road when that city became a fashionable resort in the 18th century.

Figure 96: Observatory House, home of the Herschel astronomers

Early industry arrived in the area in 1442, when Slough was chosen as the site of a major brickworks to supply bricks for the building of Eton College. Two and a half million bricks were produced there over a nine year period. Four hundred years later, in 1845, a brickworks was re-established at Slough by Thomas Nash in what is now the Diamond Road area. This encouraged the opening of the Slough arm of the Grand Union Canal in 1882, making transportation of the bricks much easier. The firm became H and J Nash Ltd, the most important brickworks in Buckinghamshire producing 14 million bricks annually from the extensive brickfields north of Slough Station. However, hospitality was always the town's main industry.

By the 1580s, there were regular coach services travelling westward out of London and Slough became one of their major stopping points. Alehouses and coaching inns quickly developed to meet the every need of their passengers. The Crown and the Reindeer were established by 1618 and were soon followed by the White Hart and the Red Lion. By the time the number had grown to seven, there were still only a total of about thirty houses in the village. Coaches travelling through had wonderful names like the Flying Machine, the Monarch, Triumph and Defiance. By the reign of King William IV in the early 19th century, 60-80 coaches a day could be seen in Slough and its importance was boosted by the establishment of a receiving house for letters (forerunner of a post office) at the White Hart Inn around 1830.

From the 18th century, the area became a fashionable place for richer individuals to build themselves country villas near Windsor and Eton. The best known of these people were Sir William Herschel and his sister Caroline, the astronomers who discovered Uranus in 1781 from their house in Bath. They lived at Observatory House in Windsor Road where Sir William built himself a vast 20ft long telescope in the garden. Georgian Society was fascinated by his work and visitors included, not only various members of the British Royal family, but also the monarchs of France, Russia and Austria. King George III, while looking through Herschel's telescope, once remarked to the Archbishop of Canterbury, "My Lord Archbishop, let me show you the way to Heaven!". The house was scandalously demolished in 1963 and a modern office block of the same name, along with a small Herschel memorial, now stands on the site.

The residential development of Slough began in earnest after the Great Western Railway between Paddington and

Maidenhead was opened in 1838. However, at first there was only a request stop at Slough, with tickets sold at the Crown Inn. The first station (slightly to the east of the present 1882 building) was not built until 1840 due to opposition from Eton College. It was grander than other such buildings because it acted as the royal station until the Windsor stations were opened in 1849.

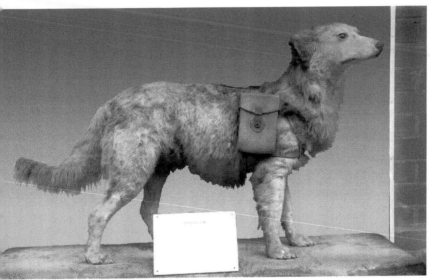

Figure 97: Station Jim at Slough Railway Station

Three years after the opening of the railway station, the first electro-magnetic public telegraph in the World was installed in a small cottage nearby. It enabled the Queen to announce the birth of her son, Prince Alfred, to the people of London within 11 minutes in 1844. The following year, a certain John Tawell poisoned his lover in Salt Hill and fled to London via Slough Station. However, he was quickly taken into custody when his description was sent via telegraph to Paddington while he was still on the train.

The most beloved fixture at Slough Station is 'Station Jim': a small stuffed dog displayed in a glass case on Platform 5. He only lived for three years from 1894-6, but in that short time became well known to commuters. He did tricks and collected money for the Great Western Railway Widows and Orphans Fund using a collecting box on his back. He would bark whenever a coin was placed in it.

A fine 'Royal Hotel' was built opposite the early station, but it closed in 1852. After standing empty for some years, the British Orphan Asylum moved into the building in 1863. This was a rather desirable residence for one's orphaned relatives and only children of respectable families were admitted by election or by the payment of a rather large lump sum of money. In later years the building was expanded and was even given its own swimming pool. It merged with another charity in 1920 and moved away. The building became the Licensed Victuallers' School until it was demolished in 1938 and a new building erected in the grounds. The school has been located in North Ascot since 1989.

After the opening of the railway, the population of the town almost doubled in ten years. St Mary's Church had been built in 1835 to serve their spiritual needs, but unfortunately it did not have the proper rights of marriage and many early weddings there turned out to be invalid. The High Street, which once had picturesque trees down the middle of its western end, became a hive of retail activity to complement the hostelries. From 1850, a popular cattle market was held weekly in William Street on Tuesdays. A town hall was built in 1887 and the area was consolidated as an urban district in 1894. This was subsequently enlarged in 1900, 1931 and 1995. The town was made a municipal borough with a royal charter in 1938 and transferred to Berkshire in 1974.

Figure 98: Slough High Street showing the Old Crown Hotel circa 1910

The brickworks were joined by other enterprises such as ironmongery and engineering manufacturing (established 1815), carriage manufacture and export, ointment production and nursery plants. James Elliman (who funded Salt Hill Park) started producing embrocations for aching and sprained muscles (for horses and dogs as well as humans) in 1847. The factory in Chandos Street exported its products all over the World between 1870 and 1961. The product is said to have become so famous because, unusually for the time, the firm spent half their profits on advertising and are even credited with having been the first company to use a cartoon strip in their adverts. Horlicks later took them over and the old factory building was eventually replaced by the Queensmere Shopping Centre. However, Elliman's Embrocation is still available from GlaxoSmithKline.

The Royal Nurseries, flanking Wexham Road with a High Street frontage, were founded by Thomas Brown in 1774. In

1845, they were purchased by Charles Turner who made Slough famous for its roses and carnations and popularized the Cox's Orange Pippin apple from Colnbrook. He advised Charles Darwin on the cross-breeding of hollyhocks and was well known in horticultural circles as the 'King of Florists'.

The town's population doubled again upon the arrival of mass employment on the Slough Trading Estate in the 1920s. The later poet laureate, John Betjeman, did not much appreciate this industrial development and, in 1937, wrote his famous, but somewhat insulting, poem beginning, "Come, friendly bombs and fall on Slough. It isn't fit for humans now". Since the mid-20th century, Slough has become one of the most successful and enterprising homes to migrant workers in Britain. Poles and Ukrainians moved to the town after the Second World War, followed by families from the Caribbean, India and Pakistan in the early 1950s. Around the same time, many families moved to Slough from London as well. Numerous older buildings in the town centre were demolished when it was redeveloped between 1964 and 1979; but the landscape has gained some interesting new architecture such as the town's first purpose-built mosque erected in Diamond Road in 1983-5.

For Slough Trading Estate, see Britwell and Manor Park

Spital and Frogmore

Spital spans the old parish boundary between Windsor and Clewer. It is named after the medieval hospital of St Peter-without-Windsor that once stood in the area: a small religious house, with a chapel, that tended to the needs of local lepers, both male and female. It was probably established in the early

13th century. When leprosy declined, Edward IV gave the place to Eton College. Long after the original foundation was gone, in 1874, Spital gained another little Arts-and-Crafts chapel dedicated to St Agnes, which is now a music centre. It may have been designed by Henry Woodyer. Just to the north, the church of All Saints was designed by Thomas Hardy, the author, whose formal career was in architecture.

Figure 99: The Royal Mausoleum and Cemetery at Frogmore

The Combermere Barracks, originally called the Clewer Barracks, were built in St Leonard's Road for the Royal Horse Guards in 1800-04. In 1869, they were rebuilt and renamed in honour of Field Marshal Lord Combermere. They are currently the home of the Household Cavalry, who are due to move out to Wiltshire imminently.

The manor of Clewer Brocas – owned by the prominent medieval family of the same name – probably covered this area. The Brocas family were important court officials who needed to be near Windsor Castle. When the Gascon, Arnold Brocas, was killed at the Battle of Bannockburn in 1314, the King took on the wardship of his three sons. The eldest, Sir John, bought his Clewer manor and other local lands soon afterwards, including the Brocas Field in Eton. He was much favoured by Kings Edward II and III. The latter appointed him Chief Forester of Windsor Forest (like the modern Ranger) and he fought for the King at the Battle of Crécy.

Sir John's son and heir, Sir Bernard, grew up with the Black Prince and the two became great friends. The Prince even tried to pair Bernard up with his royal cousin, the widowed 'Fair Maid of Kent,' until he decided to marry her himself. Sir Bernard was appointed Queen's Chamberlain under Richard II and was buried under a fine effigial monument in Westminster Abbey in 1395. After his son and namesake was executed in 1400 for opposing King Henry IV, the family fortunes were much reduced and they took to their country retreat at Beaurepaire in Sherborne St John near Basingstoke, eventually selling off Clewer in 1499.

To the south and east of Spital, were other country estates, now subsumed by the Great and Home Parks. The north-western portion of Windsor Great Park, adjoining Queen Anne's Gate, is officially called the Moat Park. It is named after the, now dry, moat of a medieval manor house purchased by King Henry VI. The Park Lodge was later built further south and, in the 18th century, an elegant 'pleasure pavilion' was built on the island in the moat. It was a kind of summer-house in which the Royals could dine, relax or just play cards. Much of the area was taken into agricultural use with the building of the Flemish Farm in 1791 in order to remove the wildlife which had encouraged poaching there. It was originally meant to follow the Flemish system of farming: hence the name.

On the far side of the Great Park Road is the Frogmore Estate, now part of the Home Park. The present Frogmore House was built in the early 18th century as a present for Queen Charlotte. She and her daughters used it as a retreat for "painting, drawing, needlework, japanning, reading and 'botanising'". Nearby is the royal mausoleum to Queen Victoria and Prince Albert and the lesser known one to Victoria's mother, the Duchess of Kent. Also buried in the royal cemetery there are King Edward VIII and the Duchess of Windsor (formerly Mrs Wallis Simpson).

Figure 100: The ghost of Herne the Hunter near Frogmore

Frogmore and Datchet Mead, adjoining the old Datchet Ferry, are mentioned in William Shakespeare's 'Merry Wives of Windsor'. Hiding in a washing basket, Falstaff was taken down to Datchet Mead and thrown, unceremoniously, into the Thames. This meadow was a busy place, where washing was bleached and dried, until the closure of the paths across the

Home Park in 1848. In medieval and Tudor times, the ferry was the most important and lucrative Thames crossing out of Windsor on the route to London. It sometimes saw huge royal entourages crossing. King Henry VIII used the meadow for horseracing and this was reinstated by King Charles II in the 1680s.

Just north of Frogmore, in the middle of the Home Park, stands the famous Herne's Oak of the Berkshire county crest, also referenced by Shakespeare. Mad King George III ordered the original tree pulled down in 1796 but it was replanted in 1906. It was supposedly the hanging tree of one Herne, the favourite huntsman of King Richard II. He nearly died saving the King's life but was framed for poaching and cast out of office. In a mad frenzy, he ran through the Forest, with antlers on his head, before hanging himself from the tree. His mounted ghost still rampages across the night's sky in a 'wild hunt' searching for lost souls across the Great Park. His name and his antlered state suggest a connection with Cernunnos the Celtic horned god of the countryside, who was also associated with oak trees.

Sunningdale

Essentially meaning Sunna's Valley, this place-name actually derives from Sunninghill Dale. It was one of the outposts of the followers of the supposed Anglo-Saxon chief, Sunna, whose settlements were centred on Sonning. They carved themselves a little village out of the wilds of Windsor Forest, always a risky area in which to live and even more so to travel through. Chobham Common and Bagshot Heath once stretched over much of Sunningdale. They were well known for bandits and were frequented by highwaymen as late as the early 19th century. The notorious Captain Snow is still commemorated in the name of Snow's Ride. The village has always relied on the local transportation routes for its prosperity: from the London to Silchester road of Roman times, later known as the Devil's Highway, to the modern A30.

Figure 101: Northcote House at Sunningdale Park

Broomhall Farm stands on the southern edge of Sunningdale in an area that was once a detached part of Sunninghill. It replaces a little known and, for much of its life, a rather a poor nunnery called Bromhall Priory. It was founded in the 12th century as a daughter house of Chertsey Abbey. The name is now sometimes used for the houses around Sunningdale Station, although this is mostly considered core Sunningdale despite only being absorbed into Berkshire from Surrey in 1995. The station, opened in 1856, was first called Broomhall Station and later Sunningdale and Windlesham Station.

The parish church, at the centre of the old village of Sunningdale, is somewhat more recent than the priory. The village was formerly in the southern portion of Old Windsor parish and villagers had to travel up to the church in Old Windsor until 1840. The present building was put up between 1860 and 1887, with Sunningdale becoming its own parish in 1894. The church is best known for its monument to Queen Victoria's half-nephew, the German Prince Victor of Hohenlohe-Langenburg. He was a well-known 19th century sculptor who, under the name of Count Gleichen (which was actually his wife's title), modelled such pieces as King Alfred's statue in Wantage. He had run away from school in his native land and was sponsored to enter the Royal Navy by the Queen. He eventually became an admiral, before turning to more artistic means of earning a living whilst in retirement. He lived at St Bruno House in Charters Road.

Figure 102: The Dormy House Ladies' Golf Club, Sunningdale

The original Charters (1868), named after the pond there, was one of several smaller country houses built in the area after the arrival of the railway. It was replaced in 1936-8 by an extraordinary white and cubic modernist building in the stripped classicist style, although the interiors are Georgian revival. It was built for Frank Parkinson, Chairman of the Crompton Parkinson electrical engineering company, and has been called the "last of the great country houses". His widow briefly lent the house to the Duke and Duchess of Windsor in 1947. Charters School was built on part of the estate in 1958. The house later became the home of Vickers Aircraft Research and then De Beers Industrial Diamonds before being turned into apartments in 2005-8.

Other houses have older origins. Sunningdale Park is a Civil Service College. The Georgian-style mansion at its centre is now known as Northcote House and is used as an event venue. Despite its classical style it was only built in 1931, replacing an earlier building of 1845 which itself had replaced a building of 1785. The short-lived Sunningdale Agreement over power-sharing in Northern Ireland was signed there in 1973. The Royal Berkshire Hotel was built as The Oaks for Charles Churchill, son of the 1st Duke of Marlborough, in 1705. His wife was the housekeeper at Windsor Castle. Another hotel, Coworth Park – sometimes called a manor – dates from 1776 and was home to the 17th Earl of Derby who was Secretary of State for War at the end of the First World War. Although mostly in Sunninghill parish, Tittenhurst Park, at Beggars' Bush (originally an area called Crack's Hole), dates back to 1737 and was the home of the Victorian medicine magnate and philanthropist, Thomas Holloway, founder of Royal Holloway College. It is perhaps best known as the home of John Lennon in the late 1960s and early 70s, and subsequently of Ringo Starr. The entrance can be seen on the cover of the Beatles' Hey Jude album and the interior features throughout the promotional film (later used as the music video) for the song, 'Imagine,' which was recorded in the studio in the garden.

Agatha Christie lived at the house called Scotswood in Devenish Road in Sunningdale in the 1920s and then moved to Styles in Charters Road, which was named after her first mystery novels. It was from this house that she herself mysteriously disappeared for eleven days before being discovered at the Harrogate Hydro. Sunningdale Golf Course features in one of her short stories, Tommy and Tuppence Beresford's 'The Sunningdale Mystery,' originally published as part of 'Partners in Crime' in 1929. Although the entrances to the famous Sunningdale Golf Club and Sunningdale Ladies' Golf Club are now in Berkshire, most of these two golf courses are in Surrey. The ladies' club is the oldest such club in the country and originally started out at Dormy House (now a care home).

A small portion of Northern Sunningdale, on the southern shores of the Virginia Water, is within the bounds of Windsor Great Park. However, Fort Belvedere and the ruins of Leptis Magna which were erected as follies in the surrounding landscape are both over the border in Surrey.

Sunninghill and South Ascot

Sunninghill means Sunna's People's Hill referring to a supposed early Anglo-Saxon leader, Sunna, whose followers set up a small kingdom in Eastern Berkshire. Centred on Sonning, the 'province of Sunningum' is recorded as early as AD 673. The name is particularly highlighted at Sunninghill because it lay on the boundary with the adjoining kingdom of 'Surrey' (meaning the Southern Kingdom).

Figure 103: Sunninghill High Street, looking north, circa 1910

The area was originally part of Windsor Forest and the inhabitants were scattered throughout the woodland. They would only come together on Sundays at Sunninghill Church, which was first built in stone in about 1120. For much of its life it was under the control of the nunnery of Bromhall, situated on the edge of adjoining Sunningdale. It was completely rebuilt in Victorian times but one of the original Norman doorways was discovered in a garden wall and has since been restored. The church is chiefly noted for its chapel to the memory of Thomas Holloway of Tittenhurst Park, who founded nearby Royal Holloway College. He is buried in the churchyard, along with Sir Home Riggs Popham of Titness Park, the Naval Commander in charge of the expedition which claimed the Cape of Good Hope for Britain.

The house called The Cedars, next to the church was once the property of the political writer, George Ellis. His friend, Sir Walter Scott, was a frequent visitor, along with other members of literary society. Sunninghill village originally grew up to the north of the church in Silwood Park, and there was a larger settlement in the vicinity of the present house. This was the original Beggars' Bush, traditionally named from a meeting place of beggars and highway robbers. When the village was removed in the 1780s, the place-name was retained south of the Cannon Crossroads (named after the pub, now an Italian restaurant).

Much of this area was certainly open heath and woodland frequented by bandits who preyed on travellers moving west from London, as well as those leaving Windsor. The parish register contains the following entry:

"A certain highwayman, whose name we know not, attempted to rob the Salisbury Stage Coach, near Kingswick Beech in this parish, was shot with a brace of bullets by a gentleman who was in ye coach on Monday the 20th Day of March 1704 and was buried here on Wednesday following."

Throughout the 18th century however, rich gentlemen began to carve out small estates for themselves in this area. In earlier times, the manor house of Sunninghill was called Eastmore and it was located somewhere near Cheapside. After the Civil War, it was eventually purchased by a parliamentarian, John Aldridge. He became a wealthy tanner and used bark from the estate in his tannery business. In 1788, James Sibbald, a banker, purchased the place. He built a fine Georgian mansion, called Silwood House, on the other side of the park, sweeping away the villagers who lived there. This was replaced in 1876-8 by the present house, designed by Sir Alfred Waterhouse. King's Wick was another important old house, which stood at the southern end of Nell Gwynne's Avenue. An old story tells how this lady used to lodge there while attending King Charles II at Windsor Castle, but this seems to have been due to a confused memory of the Gwynne family of Frogmore.

Figure 104: The Wells Inn, made famous by its healing waters

Sunninghill began to expand as a village down the west side of Sunninghill Road on Saltershill during the early 19th century. The school was founded in 1818 next to the smithy and things expanded from there. This was due partly to the popularity of nearby Ascot Races, but largely because of the chalybeate spa at the old Wells Inn (now a pan-Asian restaurant). Since the discovery of the health-giving spring there the previous century, it was one of the prime places to be seen for Windsor's high society. In its heyday, it was as popular as Bath or Tunbridge Wells, but its clientele was much more exclusive and it was even frequented by Royalty.

South Ascot developed south of Ascot Station after it opened in 1856 and developed as an important junction in 1878, but particularly after the building of the tin St Saviour's Church in 1884. Its replacement, the present All Souls' Church, was built on Sunninghill Bog between 1897 and 1911 under the patronage of the colonial governor, Lord Stanmore. He lived at the Red House (now Index House just north of the railway line) and has a fine 17th century style monument inside the church. Other early genteel villas were built in the lower Brockenhurst Road area. During the Second World War, King Zog of Albania fled the Nazi invaders of his country and settled in Britain where he spent his time gathering support for the Albanian resistance. In 1941, he settled at Forest Ridge in South Ascot.

For Sunninghill Park, see Cheapside

Swinley, Forest Park and Crown Wood

An ancient earthwork of some kind stands on Tower Hill in Swinley. Tradition connects it with the Anglo-Saxon Lady Aedflaed, owner of the surrounding Winkfield manor until she gave it away to Abingdon Abbey in 1015. There used to be the remains a 'New Tower' there, mentioned in the 17th century.

Queen Anne and her husband loved to hunt through Windsor Forest and Swinley was one of their favourite haunts. They kept the Royal Staghounds at their kennels there and the master lived at Swinley Lodge, the centrepiece of Swinley Walke, a sub-division of the Forest. It was demolished in 1830. When the Queen became too old and heavy to ride, she created the rides throughout the Forest, so she could follow the hunt in her carriage. They were later extended by George III. He also hunted around Swinley and, in 1798 when the government were worried about a French invasion, he came to review the troops at their training camp there.

Figure 105: Logging in Swinley Woods circa 1910

South of Swinley is where Bagshot Heath once spilt over the Surrey border and stretched way into Berkshire. It was a desolate area, one of the most notorious for highwaymen and footpads, and their rotting remains could often be seen swinging in chains at Wishmoor Cross. Hence:

> *Prepared for War, now Bagshot Heath we cross*
> *Where broken gamesters oft' repair their loss.*

However, some travellers were not so badly treated. There is an old story told of the chivalrous French highwayman, Claude Duval, in which he took only £100 of £400 from a certain party on the condition that the beautiful young lady in the coach, dance with him. This tale, from the reign of King Charles II, is also claimed by Maidenhead Thicket and Hounslow Heath. On another occasion, Duval robbed Squire Roper, Master of the

Royal Buckhounds, of 50 guineas and tied him hand and foot to a tree.

Swinley was the home of one of Thomas Lawrence's secondary brickworks between 1870 and 1939. Swinley bricks were used to build Madame Tussaud's, South Hill Park, Eton College and Royal Holloway College. The site is marked by the lakes, hidden in the trees, opposite the junction of Swinley Road and Blane's Lane. Swinley Woods and Park are now part of Swinley Forest, a largely modern plantation of 2,600 acres of Scots pines that has superseded the older woodland of Windsor Forest. It produces 13,250 tons of timber a year. The naming of the housing estates of Forest Park, immediately to the west of the old medieval park pale, and of Crown Wood reflect the fact that the Forest is cared for by the Crown Estates.

Upton

In the Domesday Survey of 1086, Upton is recorded as a royal village owned by William the Conqueror (and previously King Harold). It was home to 19 villeins (tenant farmers), 5 bordars (cottage dwellers), 1 serf and their families, with 15 ploughs to work 18 hides of land. It had a mill and a fishery that produced 1,000 eels a year.

Upton first developed as a village around the church, Upton Court and Upton Court Farm and then along Upton Road to the north-east. The church of St Laurence is the mother church of Slough and dates back to the early 12th century. Its old parish of Upton-cum-Chalvey once encompassed all of central Slough. St Laurence's was nearly pulled down after it fell into disrepair in the 19th century but was saved by a local farmer. It retains an interesting 13th century Italian sculpture of the Trinity, smashed during the Reformation but since reassembled. In recent years, as the burial place of famous astronomer, Sir William Herschel of Observatory House in Slough, it has been graced with a beautiful modern planetary stained-glass memorial window. With his sister, Caroline, he discovered the planet Uranus in 1781. The churchyard is thought to have been the inspiration for Thomas Gray's 1751 poem, 'Elegy in a Country Churchyard,' said to have been written under the old yew tree there.

Figure 106: Upton Court from the Churchyard

Timbers from the magnificent Upton Court have been dated as early as 1280. It is mostly a late 15th century aisled hall-house with a fine hammer-beam roof and later 17th century alterations. Currently a children's nursery, it was built as a monastic grange and manor house belonging to the monks of Merton Priory at Colliers Wood in south-east London. There are slight remains of their fish-ponds. The place has its own priest hole for hiding illegal Tudor priests. From the early 18th century, it was owned by the Lascelles family who mostly rented it out to tenants, such as Sir Thomas Douglas Forsyth, the Anglo-Indian administrator and travel writer. In 1922, when Princess Mary was to marry Viscount Lascelles, her parents King George V and Queen Mary visited Upton Court in order to assess the possibility of it becoming the newly-weds' home but they were not impressed. The place is said to be haunted by the ghost of a frill-collared lady in white with a blood stain on her left breast.

The Red Cow Inn, just across the roundabout, is a half-timbered 16th-century building and there are other similar ones nearby. It has been a pub since 1837, replacing one of the same name across the road that had been serving pints since at least the 18th century. On the other side of the road from the Red Cow, on the edge of Herschel Park, stands The Mere (now home of the National Foundation for Educational Research), an extraordinary timber-framed Arts-and-Crafts house built in 1887 for the publisher George Bentley and later home of his son, Richard. George's father, Richard Senior, had founded their business and published, for the first time, Dickens' 'Oliver Twist' in serial form in his popular magazine, 'Bentley's Miscellany'. The records of the firm, including many letters from Dickens, Harrison Ainsworth, the Trollopes and Wilkie Collins were kept in the house until sold after Richard Junior's death in 1936.

The Bentleys had earlier lived at Upton Park, one of Slough's earliest planned housing estates built in 1842. It included Victoria Terrace and East and West Villas with beautifully laid out grounds, which now form the public park named after the Herschel family. The Park was considered a "fashionable resort for the summer months" and attracted other minor gentry and the professional classes, such as the artist, Edward Matthew

Ward and the founder of the Dictionary of National Biography, George Smith.

Not far away, Eton Union Workhouse was built in Albert Road in 1835-6 to house 450 persons. Most of the old buildings survive. Fir Tree House was the entrance block with board room and porter's lodge, as well as accommodation for overnight vagrants. In the main block, men and women were segregated on east and west wings respectively. There was a schoolhouse for children and a curfew bell that rang every night at eight o'clock. The chapel was added in the 1860s and the place became famous in 1885 when the matron, Catherine Sinkins, first grew the well-known flower, Mrs Sinkins' Pink, there. The workhouse became Upton Hospital in 1948. Upton was transferred from Buckinghamshire to Berkshire in 1974.

Waltham St Lawrence

Figure 107: Reconstruction of the Roman Temple at Weycock Hill

The earliest residents of Waltham St Lawrence seem to have lived on Weycock Hill, between the village and Kiln Green. The name stems from Weg-Cocc meaning Wayside Hillock. Despite the later appendage of the word hill, there is not much of an incline there. The 'way' would be the Roman Camlet Way, running from St Albans (Verulamium) to Silchester (Calleva) which passed close by. The hillock was probably all that remained to show where a Roman temple had once stood. This was a vast octagonal building, excavated in the late 19th century, which can still be easily identified by aerial photography. Associated finds have led to the suggestion that it was dedicated to the Roman goddess, Vesta, or her Celtic equivalent. There would have been a substantial settlement nearby, full of shops and hotels for visiting pilgrims. This is reflected in the name of the parish, Waltham. Despite alternative interpretations being popular, the name almost certainly stems from Wcalt-Ham, referring to the Dilapidated Homes of the Romans that the incoming Anglo-Saxons discovered. St Lawrence is the church dedication: hence the village's ancient alternative name of Lawrence Waltham.

Traditionally, the north doorway of the church is called the Devil's Door. It is said that when the vicar enters the church's south door, the Devil exits through the north and into his shadowy side of the churchyard. Outside the southern lychgate is the old wooden pound for stray animals – a rare survival in Berkshire. The beautiful old Bell Inn nearby is also unusual for this area. It is a fine example of a medieval 'Wealden' hall-house, usually found in Sussex. It was given to the church by the prominent 16th century publisher, Ralph Newbery, who lived at Beenham's Heath. He rose to become Master of the Royal Printing House and many of the family from Waltham were subsequently publishers and booksellers in St Paul's Churchyard in London. John Newbery, a descendant of Ralph's brother, is known as the 'Father of Children's Literature' as he published the first ever range of books for children in the mid-18th century. He is particularly revered in the United States, where the John Newbery Medal is awarded each year for the "most distinguished contribution to American literature for children". He was born in Waltham St Lawrence and started out publishing the Reading Mercury newspaper in Reading Market Place before moving to London. He is buried beneath a prominent tomb chest in Waltham St Lawrence Churchyard.

Figure 108: The village pound and Bell Inn at Waltham St Lawrence

The parish registers show burials of soldiers from both sides during the Civil War, for there was supposedly a skirmish of some kind at Beenham's Heath. The village was certainly deeply divided at this time: Richard Neville, the lord of the manor, was a royalist while his own brother was a staunch parliamentarian.

The Nevilles were descendants of the Barons Bergavenny and, through them, of the great Neville family of County Durham (and Bisham). They lived at Billingbear Park, just within the southern bounds of the parish, which Henry Neville built in 1567. His son and namesake was a famous Elizabethan diplomat who had a monopoly on manufacturing British cannon. Both father and son feature on the former's fine kneeling-figured mural monument in the parish church, though their house is no more. The family are also remembered in the name of the Neville Memorial Hall, near the church: a 17th century building that was once the local schoolhouse.

In the 1920s and 30s, Milley Road became home to the Golden Cockerel Press, one of the main English quality artistic printing houses, founded by Hal Midgley Taylor in an old army surplus hut. It became famous for beautiful handmade limited editions of classic works printed on handmade paper, sometimes on vellum, with original, often wood engraved, illustrations. In 1924 the press was purchased by Robert Gibbings, an unconventional Irish wood engraver, sculptor and author who wanted to complete his latest publication at the Press. He moved to Waltham and his ownership heralded a golden age there. The Old Press (previously Four Elms) has a relief over the door by Gibbings' friend, Eric Gill. In 1933, however, production moved to Chiswick when the business was sold to three partners, including, a Francis James Newbery. Sadly, Newbery appears to have been descended from an old Devon and Dorset family with no apparent connection with the Waltham people of that name.

Warfield, Hayley Green and Newell Green

Warfield means Weir Field, a fishing place on the Cut, anciently called the How Brook. The Anglo-Saxon manor and church were probably given to the Bishopric of Winchester by Queen Emma, widow of both Kings Aethelred the Unread and Canute the Great. The Bishop may have had a house near the church but his steward probably lived in Wargrave. The old church was replaced by a new building in the 12th century but the two may have been very similar in appearance. The later church was small and narrow with an eastern apse, like similar Anglo-Saxon buildings. It has been greatly enlarged since, mostly in the 15th century, but the old Norman building still remains as the north aisle.

Figure 109: Warfield Church with one of its Green Men

Despite being much restored, the present decorated Gothic chancel is one of the medieval delights of all Berkshire churches. It has a much-damaged Easter sepulchre and a superb sedilia, highly decorated with foliage and excellent green men, that runs into the screen and relic chamber behind the altar. It was added, in about 1345, possibly for the great church patron, Sir William Trussell, whose coat-of-arms can be seen in the ancient glass; or perhaps he was just one of a number of contributors. He had lived at Foliejon Park in nearby Winkfield before moving to Shottesbrooke. During this period, the Great Plague took a terrible toll on the parish. Tradition says local people were buried in two plague pits in Hatch Lane. Two parsons certainly died in quick succession in 1350. Could they be buried under the canopied recesses in the north chapel?

This chapel has the most fantastic late medieval rood screen complete with its musicians' loft. It is usually called St Katherine's or the Staverton Chapel after the family whose memorials can be seen on its floor and walls. They lived at the main manor house in the parish: Heathley Hall at Hayley Green. Today this is called the Moat House. Its basis is a 15th century hall-house and it is still surrounded, as its name suggests, by most of the original moat. The old manor barn stands nearby at Hayley Green Farm. The house may, originally, have been the royal hunting lodge of Warfield Walke, one of the Windsor Forest sub-divisions. It was superseded in Georgian times by Warfield Grove (now Warfield House) across the road. The Rectory House, next to the church, was the home of Sir William James Herschel, the man who discovered fingerprinting. He was the grandson of Sir William Herschel the astronomer.

The Cricketers at Hayley Green is one of the better-known spots in the area. This ancient watering hole was always locally known as the Old Orchard House because of the fruit trees which surrounded it. The gamekeepers from Warfield Park are said to have frequented the inn and canny poachers would therefore always know when it was a good time to take to the woods. Nearby Newell Green, or Common, has two pub-restaurants: the Plough and Harrow and the Yorkshire Rose. Not far away is the Queen Anne style Newell Hall that was built around 1700 by the old Warfield family of Horsnaile. As well as being landowners, they dabbled in clockmaking and now have a road, spelt Horseneile, named after them in Bracknell.

Figure 110: Rough Music heard in Warfield 1874

It was past these buildings that a crowd of villagers passed, in 1874, banging their pots and pans, on the way to give the 2nd Lord Ormathwaite of Warfield Park a taste of 'rough music'. This was the traditional rural way of showing disapproval to one who had been mistreating his wife. Some four hundred locals gathered outside Warfield Park and banged about with makeshift instruments for several hours. Their ghosts are still sometimes seen on cold autumn nights.

The great house at Warfield Park no longer stands but the old park itself is now an estate of park homes. The house had been built, along with numerous grottoes, lakes and terraces by Lord Ormathwaite's ancestral uncle, Colonel John Walsh in 1766. He had made a fortune for himself in India with his friend, Lord Clive, and hoped for a quieter life in an English country retreat. His many mistresses are said to have lived at the house (but not all at once) while John partied in London. One of these ladies was a chronic depressive who apparently drowned herself in the defunct pool known as Rachel's Lake in her memory. Her ghost is said to haunt the bridge on the north side of Warfield Park, but she also runs screaming down Jigs Lane with John hot on her heels.

For Warfield Brickworks, see Wick Hill, Lawrence Hill and Quelm Park

Wargrave

The name of Wargrave is almost certainly of Ango-Saxon origin, deriving from Weir-Grove: an area of Windsor Forest, near a weir to catch fish on the River Thames. A more romantic story has the Vikings invading this part of the country in the late 9th century and fighting the local Berkshire yeomanry at this spot where they later buried their dead in a mass 'War-Grave'. The Norsemen were certainly active in the area at that time when they made Reading the headquarters for their conquest of Southern England. Queen Emma, the wife of the Anglo-Viking King Canute, is said to have had a palace at Wargrave and an old legend tells how she gave the manor to the Bishopric of Winchester in thanks for coming through an 'ordeal by fire' unscathed after she had been accused of adultery.

Wargrave Court, near the church, was the old manor house and dates from the 15th century. Queen Elizabeth I confiscated this from the Bishop of Winchester, after he annoyed her during one of his sermons, and gave it to Henry Neville of Billingbear Park. The manor remained in the family until the 19th century. The Nevilles had divided loyalties during the Civil War but Wargrave, with its growing mercantile interests, seems to have sided with the Parliament. At one point, a foraging party from the royalist garrison at Reading tried to commandeer five cartloads of wheat and a hundred and fifty sheep from Wargrave, but the villagers responded by calling in help from some passing Windsor troopers and the cavaliers were sent packing.

Figure 111: The George & Dragon at Wargrave

The present bow-fronted Wargrave Manor, immediately north of the village, is currently the English home of the Sultan of Oman. It was called Wargrave Hill when built in 1780, appropriately for lawyer Joseph Hill. In 1824, it was inherited by a distant cousin-by-marriage, Joseph Jekyll MP. His granddaughter, Gertrude, lived there with her parents for ten years in the 1870s but she did not become famous for her garden designs until after she had left the village. The building became the manor house in 1891 and changed its name 27 years later. Another well-known 18th century resident, at Barrymore House off the High Street, was the 7th Earl of Barrymore who was fostered by Reverend John Tickell, the brother-in-law of Hill's wife. Barrymore grew up to become a notorious gambler, practical joker and general party animal. He made Wargrave the toast of London society in 1791, when he built a magnificent theatre in the village at a cost of over £60,000 (about £4½m today) and installed Delphini of Covent Garden as the resident clown. King George IV was amongst the regular visitors. Unfortunately, Barrymore was accidentally shot while escorting French prisoners to Dover and, because of his vast debts, had to be hurriedly buried under the chancel of Wargrave Church.

Figure 112: Gutted Wargrave Church burnt by Suffragettes

The parish church is thought to have been founded around AD 900 on the pleasant Mill Green, where fairs were later held on All Saints' Day each year. In the mid-14th century there was also a small chapel dedicated to Corpus Christi to which a recluse, called Alan d'Ellisfield, attached his modest hermitage. Around the same time, in 1362, John Buckingham was consecrated Bishop of Lincoln at Wargrave Church. The ceremony had to take place outside the Lincoln diocese because the Dean and chapter did not approve of the appointment. Wargrave was probably chosen by the Bishop of Salisbury, whose palace was at nearby Sonning, as it was a convenient ferry crossing point over the River Thames which marked the boundary between the dioceses of Salisbury and Lincoln.

In 1707, the church was the scene of the whirlwind wedding of Frances Kendrick of Calcot Park and a poor lawyer called Benjamin Child. According to legend, the 'Berkshire Lady,' as she was later called, had taken a fancy to this young man at a wedding party. At a masked duel, she had then forced him to choose between fighting and marrying her. He chose the latter. The church is most famous for being one of the more unfortunate victims of the Suffragette Movement. The building was completely gutted by fire during a riot in 1914, the plate and parish registers (dating from 1538) being snatched from the flames. A Madame Tussaud is buried in the churchyard, a granddaughter-in-law of the famous wax worker, and there is also an interesting mausoleum and 'peace memorial' designed by Sir Edwin Lutyens. He was a frequent visitor to the Hannens of Ouseleys and Wargrave House, a family of builders who erected the east front of Buckingham Palace, Osborne House and the restored Royal Lodge.

The central area of the village is probably best known for its inns which once served the myriad of coaches travelling between Henley and Reading or Wokingham. The Bull seems to be most famous for its ghostly landlady, who howls in distress as she is evicted from her home. The George and Dragon has a superb, though now rather dark, pub sign encased in glass, which was painted by two Royal Academicians, George Dunlop Leslie and John Evan Hodgson. It is mentioned in Jerome K Jerome's 'Three Men in a Boat'. A brighter modern copy has recently been removed.

Water Oakley

The crossroads where the Windsor Road meets the Fifield Road and Monkey Island Lane is sometimes known as Builders' Cross. According to an old story, the Anglo-Saxon church of Bray parish stood there. Being some way from the village, the locals found it difficult to keep the building in good repair. By King Edward I's reign, it was almost falling down, so they agreed to build a new church. However, every time work began, evil spirits destroyed the builders' progress. Eventually, the Queen, who owned the manor (hence nearby Queen's Eyot), was called in to help. She delegated the situation to her beadle, who suggested the church site be moved to Bray. The new church supposedly had two pieces of sculpture from the old one transferred to it: one of a dog or horse can easily be seen on the outer wall of the old chantry chapel in the churchyard.

It has been suggested that the chantry sculpture originally came from a Roman temple, at Builders Cross, dedicated to Hecate. It would have been converted for Christian use by the early Anglo-Saxons. This goddess was the patroness of cemeteries and a Romano-British burial ground was discovered near Builderswell, the area around the spring that feeds the gravel pits behind the crossroads. These pits were previously a mill pond and originally a natural lake. Many broken bronze swords and spears have been recovered there, indicating a connection with the cemetery. At death, the Celts appear, like King Arthur, to have been in the habit of throwing their most prized possessions into the swirling depths of lakes or rivers. There is further evidence that, in Iron Age times, the bodies went in too. There may have been a settlement of some kind at Arbour Bridge Pasture between Down Place Farm and Builderswell. Places called Cold Harbour are associated with Roman roads and may have been local stop-over points.

Figure 113: Oakley Court, a location for many Hammer Films

The medieval area of settlement in Water Oakley was around Queen's Wharf. Windsor Forest timber, for the rebuilding of the choir roof at Westminster Abbey, was transported down river from there in 1352. The area is now the site of Oakley Court, a castellated and turreted gothic revival mansion, built in 1857 for Richard Hall-Saye. During the Second World War, it was the home of Frenchman, Ernest Olivier, the Turkish Consul in Monte Carlo. He entertained many diplomats there. Although evidence is lacking, there is a strong tradition that General De Gaulle was a frequent visitor and hence the Court is often erroneously said to have been the headquarters of the French Resistance. The house is now a luxury hotel but it is perhaps best known for its many film roles including:

- Tommy Steele's dream house in Half a Sixpence (1967)
- Jack Palance's castle in Dracula (1973)
- Tim Curry's castle in The Rocky Horror Picture Show (1975)
- Sheila Hancock's school in the Wildcats of St Trinian's (1980)

This is perhaps not surprising as the estate was carved out of the adjoining Down Place, which is the home of Bray Studios. The house was bought by Hammer Films in 1957 and was where many of their horror movies were made. Down Place house itself dates from about 1750 and was the popular meeting place of the Kit-Kat Club during the ownership of Jacob Tonson. This group of gentlemen met, around the time of King William III's death, to ensure the Protestant succession of the Crown.

Wexham Court and Upton Lea

Only a very small part of Wexham Court parish was ever historically part of the old Buckinghamshire parish of Wexham. This was the area north of the Frithe and east of Wexham Road. Upton Lea is the northern part of the old parish of Upton-cum-Chalvey. The name comes from a farm, sometimes called Upton Place, that once stood alone at what is now the entrance to Mirador Crescent, on the east side of the Wexham Road

Roundabout. From the mid-19th century, it was the home of Henry Fleetwood Nash of H and J Nash's Slough Brickworks. The Wexham Brickworks adjoining the house, where Borderside now sits, would appear to have been their earliest endeavour. Both Wexham Court and Upton Lea became part of Berkshire in 1974.

Figure 114: Wexham Park in 1861, replaced by the Hospital in 1965

Wexham Park Hospital was built in 1965 on the site of an old country house of the same name. The house was at first called Wexham Lodge and was built on the edge of Wexham Green in the very earliest years of the 19th century by Major John Bent. Wexham Green was a sizeable roadside village, stretching from the heliport off Wexham Street, across the hospital site, to the Church Lane/Wexham Park Lane junction. In 1861, Lieutenant Joseph Grote had the house completely rebuilt in neo-Elizabethan style and renamed Wexham Park, presumably sweeping away the village in the process. Having been one of Napoleon's gaolers in Plymouth and served in the First Anglo-Burmese War, he was, by this time, senior partner of the Prescott, Grote and Co Bank. The house was subsequently owned by Sir Charles Pigott, the 3rd Baronet, who had been severely wounded during the Crimean War before the Battle of Sebastopol. He took a great interest in the gardens at Wexham, which became renowned in horticultural circles.

A small part of the old settlement of Wexham Green survived around the current Post Office and the thatched cottage at the northern end of Wexham Road. Just south of this, the house currently known as Wexham Lodge had been built, also in the early 19th century. It was then called The Firs and was probably mostly rebuilt about fifty years later by a merchant trading with India called Samuel John Southey.

Slightly to the east of the Lodge was Wexham Court. This was the old manor house of Wexham, as indicated by the large medieval moat that long survived around it. However, by the early 19th century, it had degenerated into a simple farm house and was occupied by George Botham, brother of the patron of Salt Hill's Windmill Hotel. The Court was eventually superseded by Wexham Court Primary School when the Wexham Court housing estate was built in the 1950s. This area was the original Anglo-Saxon 'Wax-makers' Home' with St Mary's Church just across the road (which is still in Buckinghamshire). Perhaps they lived in the 6th and 7th century farmhouse halls excavated beneath the Oak House Care Home. They had replaced a late Bronze Age high-status roundhouse with a prominent entrance within a ditched enclosure.

White Waltham

The church at White Waltham (historically sometimes Blanche Waltham) was originally an Anglo-Saxon minster, tending to the needs of people for many miles around. The site may have been chosen due to its proximity to the old Roman temple on Weycock Hill, in adjoining Waltham St Lawrence, which could have had a Dark Age Christian successor. A large Roman villa was also found near the lake at Waltham Place. By the time the Anglo-Saxons arrived, the old Roman temple complex was in ruins, and they saw it as a Dilapidated Home or Wealt-Ham: hence Waltham. White Waltham, Shottesbrooke and Waltham St Lawrence were originally all one estate under this name.

Figure 115: Bury Court Farm at White Waltham

The principal manor in the parish, called Berry, was centred on Bury Court Farm, opposite the church. This was owned by Chertsey Abbey but rented out to tenants. The village was therefore sometimes known as Waltham Abbots, but the name based on the local white chalk eventually triumphed. At the time of the Domesday Survey (1086), the manor was leased to a certain Turold. There were several contemporaries with this name, but this one may have been the steward to Geoffrey de Mandeville, the Constable of the Tower of London. He helped him establish Hurley Priory.

Very close to Bury Court Farm, on the south side of the church, stands the 18th century Waltham Place (formerly Hill House). This is the manor house of the manor called Walthamsland, or sometimes Windsors. The old house was the home of William Neile (died 1670), the mathematician, who had his own observatory on the roof. Later, in 1744, it was purchased by James Theobald, secretary of the Royal Society and the Society of Antiquaries for many years. He was a rich timber merchant but also a keen natural historian who, through his Scandinavian contacts, was able to present the Royal Society with many specimens of fish and trees for their collections.

The famous Berkshire historian, Thomas Hearne, was born at Littlefield Green, just to the south of White Waltham village, in 1678. With the help of Squire Cherry, he gained an excellent education and became assistant keeper of the Bodleian Library at Oxford University. He is best known for his editing of

- Leland's Itinerary
- Camden's Annals
- Spilman's Life of Alfred the Great
- Fordun's Scotichronicon

In one of his works, Hearne tells an amusing story concerning the Vicar of White Waltham, one John Blower. Queen Elizabeth I had travelled over from Windsor to hear him preach, an event which the poor man most certainly did not relish. The nervous Blower addressed the lady first as "My Royal Queen" but, later, this became "My Noble Queen," at which point the monarch was heard to observe loudly, "What! Am I ten groats worse than I was?" It is said that the vicar never preached a sermon again.

The church stands on a very ancient site. The yew tree in the churchyard is 2,000 years old. The present building is mostly Victorian but retains a 14th century chequerboard transept with some interesting old graffiti on the outside. Monuments inside include those to Neile, Theobald, (a modern one to) Hearne and also to Sir Constantine Phipps (died 1723), the Lord Chancellor of Ireland who lived at Heywood Lodge with his wife's family. Just outside the churchyard are the 17th century parish stocks and whipping post.

Figure 116: The stocks and whipping post at White Waltham

The village at White Waltham is slightly further west from the church, on the edge of Shottesbrooke Park. This was the scene of the Waltham 'Smallpox Riot' of 1870. There had been a case of smallpox in Maidenhead and the Board of Health there wanted to move the affected family to a more isolated area. For some reason, they chose a cottage in the centre of White Waltham near the war memorial junction. The villagers, naturally enough, felt this quite inappropriate. Protests from the vicar fell on deaf ears, so about sixteen local men blacked-up and descended on the cottage at night with sledge hammers and iron bars. They allowed the two men preparing the place to escape but smashed doors, windows and everything in sight, whilst scattering the burning logs from the fireplaces over the floors. The cottage was rendered unusable and the village was saved but five men were arrested for rioting.

After the Second World War, White Waltham was chosen as the location for one of the satellite 'new towns' to be built around London. It was to house 60,000 people whose homes had been flattened in the Blitz and would have spread from Woodlands Park to Shurlock Row and Waltham St Lawrence to Touchen End. Luckily, the area was considered too agriculturally important and the town was moved to Bracknell instead.

Wick Hill, Lawrence Hill and Quelm Park

Wick Hill, in old Warfield parish, probably has its origins in an ancient Anglo-Saxon dairy farm. This would presumably have been on the site of Old Farm, off Old Farm Drive, whose farmhouse dates back to the late 15th century. Other old buildings also stand in this area. Five hundred years later, the lower slopes of Wick Hill became a residential area for Bracknell's gentry, and it still retains several beautiful old villas on the western side of Warfield Road. Wick Hill House in Kenilworth Avenue was the residence of the famous Victorian explorers, Clement St George Royds Littledale and his wife, Teresa. They unfortunately travelled the World in search of unusual animals to hunt. Clement's taxidermic trophies were used to decorate his Bracknell home and upon his death in 1921 were presented to the British Museum. King George V was given his prized Asiatic Ibex. He was best known, however, for his mapping expeditions and became the first European to travel many of the uninviting mountain passes of Tibet.

Figure 117: Wick Hill House, famous taxidermist's home

Warfield was once well known for its handmade brick production, and the largest and longest lived of the old brick firms, Thomas Lawrence of Bracknell (or TLB for short), was located at the top of Wick Hill, now called Lawrence Hill in his honour. The brown clay to be found in this area is ideal for making rich warm red-fired bricks. The works once produced 12 million bricks and 10 million tiles a year and they were used all around the World. Between 1860 and 1895, Lawrence's Brickworks sat between Gough's Lane and Priory Lane, around Flemish Place where the old 'settling' or 'rubber' pond can still be seen. An overhead ropeway carried the bricks from there to other parts of the works. The reconstruction of a brick chimney in the park off Goddard Way is a memorial to the brickworkers who made Warfield famous in the late 19th and early 20th centuries. There was an independent Gough's Lane Brickworks slightly further north in the angle of the roundabout between Harvest Ride and Maize Lane. It began in 1926 but was acquired by Lawrence's in 1948. Folder's Lane, in Quelm Park, was the site of another short-lived brickworks in the 1880s that straddled the road on either side. The two lakes in the Braybrooke Recreation Ground and adjoining Lakeside mark the site. The Lords Braybrooke lived at Billingbear Park in Waltham St Lawrence and owned land in this area.

The Lawrence Hill and Quelm Park housing estates were built in the late 1990s. The latter is named after the ancient Quelm Lane, a name that implies a gibbet once stood in the vicinity, perhaps where local highwaymen were hung. Quelm Lane is said to be haunted by the ghost of such a man on a white horse who children are told will steal them away if they are out late at night. Dogs will, apparently, not walk down it in the dark.

Windsor

Windsor is of course best known for its castle, home of the British monarchy for almost a thousand years, and the largest inhabited castle in the World. Legend suggests that it was built on the site of a Celtic encampment, where King Arthur or one of his subordinates lived. The town is certainly mentioned in Arthurian literature. Traditionally, the Round Table stood atop the motte of the Round Tower. In reality, it was William the Conqueror who picked the site (which was then in the manor of Clewer) for a defensive wooden motte and bailey castle, built soon after 1066. It wasn't until a few generations later that the Castle replaced Old Windsor as a royal palace as well. The name, meaning Winch-furnished-Riverbank, was even transferred there too. The Castle was totally rebuilt in stone during the 12th and 13th centuries, when it became a particularly popular residence of the English kings.

Figure 118: The Guildhall whose columns don't touch the floor above

With such an obvious centre for royal patronage and the associated supply trade, the settlement of Windsor quickly grew up between the Castle and the Thames. Activities at the Castle would swell its population at times, with builders, retainers, pilgrims or, of course, soldiers, particularly during three sieges in the dangerous political times of its early years: 1193, 1216 and 1263. Windsor's right to hold a market, dating from before 1261, reveals the place's status as an early town. At this date, it is recorded that the townsfolk guarded their privileges so zealously that they attacked several Reading merchants who were trying to muscle in on their territory. The poor men from Reading were physically assaulted and had their goods trampled in the mud. Free Borough status, with a merchant guild to supervise local crafts and trade, was not officially granted until 1277.

Figure 119: Edward III's lover drops her garter at a Windsor Ball

As well as advantages, this charter brought unwanted residents to the town: for the County Gaol was set up in Windsor. The townsfolk objected but to no avail until 1309 when there was a gaol-break and several prisoners sought sanctuary in the parish churchyard. They were captured by force of arms and were either killed in the skirmish or hanged soon afterwards. King Edward II later deemed it prudent to remove the gaol to Wallingford. In the 13th century, the town also had a thriving Jewish community. They were forced out by officialdom in 1283, although this is recorded to have been "without doing them injury". A Steward of the Guild was introduced alongside the existing two bailiffs in 1336 and a mayor by 1363, after which the two offices rapidly merged. What we would today call the local council was then the 'fraternity' run by 30 aldermen, benchers, burgesses and brethren.

Once well-known landmarks in Windsor have now long since disappeared. The medieval market cross (rather like those still to be seen today in places like Chichester and Salisbury) was erected at the castle gates in 1380. Being at the intersection of several major roads in the town, it was a popular meeting place. Not far away stood the old open-arcaded market hall, in the middle of the High Street. Today's Guildhall was built in a similar style almost on the same spot in 1687-90, by the Castle's master mason, John Clark, under the direction of Sir Thomas Fitch. Fitch died before it was finished and, in theory, Sir Christopher Wren took his place. However, despite subsequent claims, he does not seem to have actually been involved at all. Stories of Wren building the hotel named after him also appear to be unfounded, but he was both the son and nephew of a Dean of Windsor and spent much of his childhood in the town. In 1829, the columns on the east side of the Guildhall were removed and an extension erected in their place by local builder James Bedborough. An old story tells how the burgesses of Windsor were so worried by this loss of support below the Guildhall's upper rooms that they insisted he insert some extra columns. Bedborough complied but, to justify his confidence in his original design, he left a gap so the pillars would not reach the upper floor they were supposed to support.

King Edward I was the first to make Windsor Castle a real family home for the Royals. He held his coronation feast at the castle in 1275, with jousting in the surrounding park, and four of his children were born within its walls. The tone changed in King Edward III's reign when the Castle became the centre of preparations for the Hundred Years' War in France. The town would have been filled with armourers, blacksmiths and carpenters. Later, many prisoners from the King's wars, including foreign Royalty, were held at Windsor:

- King David II of Scots (1346-57): Most of his imprisonment was spent in London and Odiham (Hampshire). Ransom 100,000 marks (£66,666 13s 4d), only a few instalments of which were ever paid.
- King John II of France (1356-60): He was also lodged at Hertford, Somerton, the Tower and the Savoy. Ransom 3,000,000 crowns. He later returned to England when he was unable to complete the ransom payments.
- And, later, King James I of Scots (1420-24): He courted Jane Beaufort (daughter of John Beaufort, Earl of Somerset and granddaughter of Prince John of Gaunt, Duke of Lancaster) there and wrote 'The King's Quair' about his love for her. Ransom 60,000 marks (£40,000).

From 1351, King Edward III had his architect, William of Wykeham, Bishop of Winchester, almost totally rebuild Windsor Castle. This was originally under the watchful eye of three local friends: the Constable, Thomas Foxley of Foxley Green (Touchen End), and his assistants, Oliver de Bordeaux of Foliejon (Winkfield) and John Brocas of Clewer Brocas (Spital). It is said that this rebuilding was inspired by the royal prisoners who had complained about their surroundings and thus encouraged the King to reconstruct his palace – and their ransoms paid for it. Edward also wanted a new home for his foundation, the Order of the Garter: an exclusive chivalric club for his closest friends. It was so named after the King's supposed lover, the 'Fair Maid of Kent,' dropped her garter at a Windsor ball. The monarch was obliged to insist his knights did not use this as an excuse to think unkindly of her and the Order made sure they remembered. In these years of plague, there were few workmen available and builders were apparently press-ganged into coming to Windsor from all over the country. On completion of the building work, King Edward and Wykeham walked through the Castle together and the King noticed a Latin inscription carved in the new stonework that he translated as "Wykeham made me". The King, who had commissioned the work, was incensed but the wily Bishop quickly explained that it really said, "I was the making of Wykeham".

Figure 120: The gates to Edward IV's Chantry in St. George's Chapel

Berkshire does not have a cathedral, but St George's Chapel in Windsor is grander than many cathedrals. The first Chapel Royal within the walls of the castle was built by King Henry III and later enlarged by Edward III, in 1363, as a collegiate chapel of canons. St George, as the country's new patron saint, was chosen for the dedication. He was neither Norman nor Anglo-Saxon, so could unite a divided England. Over the years, the place became a great centre for the worship of holy relics, which further boosted visitor numbers in the town. Whilst on campaign in 1282, King Edward I captured a Welsh cross reliquary containing part of the Crucifixion Cross and, by 1352, it was at Windsor. The Holy Roman Emperor Sigismund made a gift of St George's heart in 1416 and this was later joined by his arm, two fingers and part of his skull. The Royal Chapel's large collection of other relics were mostly kept in little niches in the huge reredos (or screen) behind the High Altar.

Figure 121: Did Shakespeare write plays at the Garter Inn?

The masterpiece of high medieval Gothic architecture that we see at St George's today was erected in front of the original building by King Edward IV in the late 1470s. It was a rival to Eton College Chapel, just over the River, which had been erected by his old Wars of the Roses enemy and predecessor Henry VI. It would have been the family mausoleum of the Yorkist Kings, had they lasted. Both men were buried at St George's, although only King Edward's chantry gates survive

Henry VI's body had been transferred from Chertsey Abbey when it became clear that the saintly monarch's remains were also attracting generous pilgrims. A later draw was the body of the 14th century Rev. John Schorne, transferred from North Marston in Buckinghamshire. He was famous for having 'conjured the Devil into a boot".

Edward IV also created the Home Park, below the castle walls. It was originally the site of the Anglo-Saxon village of Orton but, by his time, had become common land, known as Underore Field. As it was so close to the Castle, the King decided to empark it for hunting deer in 1467. In Elizabethan times, there was a 'standing' there from which invited spectators could watch the deer being hunted by the privileged. In the reign of King Charles II, spectacular military re-enactments were performed there, such as the Siege of Maastricht by the French.

The 15th century had brought the 'pestilence' to Windsor and, afterwards, the place was described as "emptied and wasted" but things recovered during the Tudor period. There were many royal gatherings and processions that brought prosperity, like the visit of Duke Philip of Burgundy or the honeymoon of Queen Mary Tudor and King Philip of Spain. The religious turmoil of King Henry VIII's reign impacted heavily on Windsor. In 1536, during the Dissolution of the Monasteries, two Windsor men were hanged for their overtly Roman Catholic beliefs. A local priest was accused of supporting the revolutionary 'Pilgrimage of Grace'. He was hanged on a tree near Windsor Bridge after implicating a local butcher who then suffered the same fate at the Castle Gate. Local tradition suggests the two bodies were then displayed from the top of the Curfew Tower. Towards the end of Henry's reign, however, it was zealous Protestants who were being martyred in the town. Anthony Pearson was a popular local preacher, Henry Filmer a churchwarden and Robert Testwood a lay clerk at St George's Chapel. They were three unlucky members of a larger Protestant movement in Windsor who were rounded up, arrested and publicly burnt to death near the plaque that commemorates them next to the King George V Memorial Fountain in Datchet Road.

Figure 122: Windsor circa 1670, including maypole and the windmill

William Shakespeare is said to have written his 'Merry Wives of Windsor' at the behest of Queen Elizabeth I when she wished to see Sir John Falstaff (from 'Henry IV') in love. Traditionally it was first performed in the Chapter Library of the Castle around 1597, although this may have been an unofficial preview. The play features many local landmarks. The bard had Falstaff stay at the Garter Inn. A replacement building is now part of the Hart and Garter in the High Street: two inns combined as one. Shakespeare probably stayed there himself on many occasions while researching his play. His characters, Mistresses Ford and Page, were certainly from local families and the Ford house was said to be one of the buildings demolished from beneath the Castle wall almost opposite the Hart and Garter.

Falstaff's good-humoured host at the Garter Inn may have been based on the real owner, Richard Gallys Junior, the son of the local MP. His father, Richard Gallys Senior, has a prominent heraldic memorial board in St John's Church, though the brass featuring his large family probably disappeared during the rebuilding of 1820-22. Gallys Senior was supposedly bewitched, and ultimately killed, by a local coven of five witches from Windsor and Clewer in 1574. They were led by a certain Mother Seidre from Paynall's Almshouse in Sheet Street and each had their own 'familiar': a cat, a rat or a toad. They were eventually arrested on suspicion of plotting to murder the Queen, were gaoled at Reading, tried at Abingdon and burnt to death.

King Charles I was not a popular man in Windsor during the years prior to the Civil War. The House of Commons showed concern that he was raising forces at the Castle "without the consent of Parliament" and there was rioting in the town. Despite his hopes of making Windsor his headquarters, the King decided it was more prudent to move north. Shortly after he left, Prince Rupert bombarded the town for seven hours using five cannon stationed at Eton. During the War, Parliament placed the Castle in the charge of Colonel Venn. Troops were billeted throughout the town by the thousand, and Lord Fairfax and Oliver Cromwell were frequent visitors while training their New Model Army in the Home Park. Royalist prisoners populated the castle. The Colonel initially stabled horses in St George's Chapel but was later commanded by Parliament to "take care that there be no disorders and disturbances made in the Chapel at Windsor". Despite this, many windows and monuments were smashed and furnishings looted. So much so that after the King's execution, his fellows found it difficult to find a suitable resting place for him amongst the chaos in the Chapel. Much survived destruction, however, as did the Castle itself, to be restored and added to during the reigns of Kings Charles II, George III, George IV and Queen Victoria until the building we see today was created. It is hard to believe that, after the Civil War, the Castle was very nearly pulled down. The bill in Parliament was defeated by just one vote.

King Charles II greatly favoured Windsor Castle in the summer months when the town was teeming with courtiers and up to 300 soldiers were housed in local inns before Windsor officially became a garrison town. An old story, for which there is sadly no evidence, tells that Charles' mistress, Nell Gwynne, often stayed at the house now named after her in Church Street and would visit her lover in the Castle down a secret underground passage. After the birth of their first son, Charles Beauclerk, Earl of Burford (later Duke of St Albans), the King did build Nell a vast mansion – called Burford House – in St Albans Street. It had a beautifully decorated staircase by Antonio Verrio, the man who introduced Baroque mural painting to England.

In the early 18th century, Kings George I and II preferred their outer London palaces to Windsor Castle but the town managed to survive through the patronage of the St Albans family and other local gentry. However, it did also gain something of a reputation as a 'scoundrel town'. The second finest house in Windsor at this time was on the corner of Peascod and William Streets. Pilgrim Place (since demolished) was the home of Richard Topham the Keeper of the Records at the Tower of London. He was a very rich collector of books, prints and drawings which he left to Eton College. His eventual heir was the very successful fortune-hunter, Lord Sidney Beauclerk.

Figure 123: The Queen's Lodge alongside Windsor Castle

In 1777, the Queen's Lodge was built adjoining the Castle and the Royal family returned to Windsor. George III became well known in the area and was often seen riding his horse or shopping in the town. Retail businesses began to boom again and the population quickly doubled in size. Of particular note was the Queen's milliner, Mrs Caley, who set up on Castle Hill, with her shop moving to the High Street in 1823. It continued as a department store of the John Lewis partnership until its closure in 2006. Queen Victoria also made Windsor her home and a place for state visits. She was, however, less keen on it after the death of Prince Albert. The Prince Consort's typhoid may have been contracted in Windsor, where there was an epidemic due to open sewers and cess pits in the poorer quarters. Like his children, he had been a great patron of various institutions and projects in the town. He had even introduced the first Christmas Tree in England to the Castle. In 1848, he negotiated the opening of two railway stations in Windsor. This massively encouraged the tourism that still feeds the town's economy to this day.

Winkfield, Maiden's Green and Nuptown

The name Winkfield comes from Wineca's Field, Wineca being a man's name meaning Little Friend. In AD 942, when the village was owned by a nun named Saethryth, the parish boundary was the subject of a detailed charter. This document identified such places as Bracknell, Black Moor (around Burleigh/North Ascot) and Chawridge Manor Farm. The original 13th century manor house at the latter place probably stood within one of the old moats to be found at Maiden's Green. It was owned by the nuns of Bromhall Priory until St John's College, Cambridge took it on at the Dissolution of the Monasteries. They appointed Thomas Warde, Keeper of Cranbourne Chase, to look after it.

Figure 124: The White Hart opposite Winkfield Church

Maiden's Green probably refers to a 'New Green' which later developed at Chawridge, perhaps in the mid-17th century. Handpost Farm dates from 1630. The core area of this hamlet has always been around the two road junctions between Cock's Lane and Church Road. The Winning Post has been a pub, mostly known as the Jolly Farmer, since the 1880s, although the building may date from the 1470s. The recently demolished Crown and Anchor had been a pub and later a restaurant since at least the 1840s and Stirrups, once called the Jolly Gardener, since at least 1850. Bailey's Garage was named after a saddler called George Bailey who was living there as early as 1907. The settlement once had its own windmill just to the west, as the name Windmill Hill reminds us. Nearby Nuptown is a corruption of Up-Town. The hamlet includes Nuptown House, a hall-house dating back to around 1500.

In 1540, Richard Warde, the son of the Chawridge manor steward, was granted the manor of Winkfield, but he preferred to live at Hurst near Wokingham, where he built himself a fine house: Hurst House. During the patronage of the next generation of Wardes, the old 14th century parish church underwent sweeping changes in 1592. This is when the extraordinary row of wooden pillars was installed down the middle of the nave, so that bride and groom have to weave in and out as they return from the altar. An old story tells how the rebuilding work was hampered by the Devil until it was agreed that he could build the northern half himself. The columns were used to demark which side was his. The church also houses a very interesting twelfth century shaft piscina with intricate carving, including a horn-blowing Windsor Forest huntsman.

The 17th century White Hart Inn, on the other side of the road, used to be the local Court House. Judge Jeffreys is said to have once sat in judgment there. The Wardes' manor house, called Godwins, also stood somewhere in this area, but they would have rarely visited and it probably fell into disrepair during the time of their successors, the royalist Harrisons. In 1652, during the Commonwealth, the confiscated manor was sold off and divided up.

Figure 125: Foliejon Park, named after an unfortunate encounter

There are a number of other great houses in the northern section of the parish. One of the best known is the third manor in Winkfield, at Foliejon. The present house on the hill dates from 1801. It was the home of the exiled King Haakon VII of Norway during the Second World War. The original moated manor down on the Drift Road, once called Bellestre, was the early 14th century Berkshire home of John de Drokensford, the Bishop of Bath and Wells, who needed a base near to the Royal Court at Windsor. He may have been the one to promote the holy well of St Hubert, in the grounds, as a cure for eye complaints. The manor's name is said to have changed when a certain lady of the manor discovered her footman in flagrante delicto with one of the village wenches. She apparently exclaimed, "This is folly, John!". It is more likely, however, that the extravagant bishop built an early folly at his Berkshire manor, for the lands were eventually seized by the King as security against Drokensford's mounting debts. The deer park surrounding it was enclosed in the early 14th century by Oliver de Bordeaux, one of King Edward II's Gascon favourites. He held the manor as his main residence in return for the rent of a single red rose. It later passed to his step-son, Sir William Trussell, but King Edward III wanted to attach the park to Windsor Great Park and soon forced William to swap it for Eaton Hastings, near Faringdon. He later made his home at Shottesbrooke. Not far from Foliejon is the Neo-Tudor-Gothic New Lodge, built in 1857 for the Belgian Ambassador, Jean-Sylvain Van de Weyer. The previous house had been the home of Princess Sophia of Gloucester.

In the 19th century, an old lady lived in Winkfield who was generally thought to be a witch. One story is told of how a man who borrowed her spectacles and failed to return them, found that the lady turned herself into a squirrel and pelted him with nuts. Later, when a number of workmen made too much noise in an adjoining house, she became a hare and made trouble around the worksite. One of the labourers, however, brought his dog to work and set it on the rodent. The hare got a bloodied leg and barely escaped with its life by jumping through the window of the witch's house. Spying on the old lady later that evening, the workmen saw her nursing her wounded leg by the fire.

Woodlands Park

Despite being in White Waltham parish, Woodlands Park is now firmly attached to the suburbs of Maidenhead. A Roman cemetery, perhaps associated with the temple on Weycock Hill, was discovered beneath the railway there. Later the area became part of the manor of Heywood or West Waltham. This was centred on Heywood Lodge, originally the site of a grange of Waltham Abbey in Essex. Although both places had the same name, this appears to have been pure coincidence. Perhaps it was felt appropriate that Waltham Abbey should own land at Waltham in Berkshire. It seems to have been called West Waltham because it was west of the abbey; although it is, of course, the eastern part of the parish. Heywood was one of the Domesday (1086) manors of White Waltham. Before the Norman Conquest, it was owned by King Harold and, as Herwood is an early form, the name is believed to derive from Harold's Wood.

Figure 126: Heywood Lodge which stood on the site of Woodlands Park

In the late 13th century, a local Berkshire man, Reginald o: Maidenhead, was Abbot of Waltham. He erected some illega gallows in Cannon Lane and, in 1275, hanged a woman there

She was reputedly a local witch, accused of practising the black arts by the Abbot himself, who had some sort of grudge against her. Local – probably retrospective – legend says the woman cursed the area where she died. There were certainly seven successive horrible deaths that occurred in the village and on the railway line early this century. This culminated in the murder of Gwendoline Warren, whose case became so notorious that the village had to change its name. Once called Heywood Park, the place became known as Woodlands Park, and the deaths ceased.

In the 17th century, Heywood Lodge was the home of Sir Robert Sawyer, the Attorney-General and Speaker of the House of Commons, who prosecuted the Rye House Plotters for attempting to assassinate King Charles II. The poetess Duchess of Wellington was born there in 1889. The house stood where Lower Phipps Close is today, just east of the playground. Part of its moat, which remained in good condition right up to the 1950s, ran along the boundary at the back of the properties on the north side of Heywood Avenue.

White Waltham Airfield adjoins Woodlands Park. It was created in 1928 for the De Havilland family's Flying School. It was taken over by the Government in 1938 and became the home of the Air Transport Auxiliary during the Second World War. The aircraft manufacturer, Fairey Aviation, tested their planes there from 1947 to 1964 and Prince Philip learnt to fly here in 1952. The airfield finally passed out of RAF hands in 1982 and is now the home of the West London Aero Club.

Wraysbury and Sunnymeads

This parish of Wraysbury became part of Berkshire in 1974. A tripled-ditched enclosure excavated near Wraysbury Primary School may have surrounded an old Roman temple, although it may equally have been a simple cattle pen. However, the settlement is basically Anglo-Saxon. Wraysbury was spelled Wyrardisbury until relatively modern times. It is an Anglo-Saxon name, usually taken to mean Wigric's Fort, although the prefix could alternatively refer to weirs on the Thames. It is suggested that the suffix refers to a lesser Anglo-Saxon royal complex, on the site now occupied by King John's Hunting Lodge (alias Place Farm), off Old Ferry Road. It would have been just across the ferry from the similarly dated palace excavated near Old Windsor Church. The current lodge is a late 15th century timber-framed house, incorporating an aisled hall with two-storey jettied porch. As its name suggests, it is supposed to have been an old royal hunting lodge – not necessarily for King John – and the proposed earlier building may have served the same purpose. It eventually became the manor house of Remenham's.

At the time of the Domesday Survey (1086), the village was owned by Robert Gernon, the Duke of Boulogne. His main English home was Mountfitchet Castle at Stansted (Essex), but Wraysbury was more convenient for Windsor. The village was relatively large with 32 villeins (tenant farmers), 18 bordars (cottage dwellers), 7 serfs and their families. There were also 4 fisheries, 2 mills and woodland for 500 pigs, but no mention of a church. St Andrew's Church dates back to the 13th century but evidence of mid-Saxon occupation has been found in the immediate surrounding area. The manor house probably stood on the site of the present Manor Farmhouse, just to the north of the church. This is a late 18th century rebuild of a late medieval timber-framed house. The nearby George Inn dates back to the 16th century and was anciently used as a kind of village hall.

Figure 127: The Baptist Church and Perseverance Pub at Wraysbury

One of the two Domesday mills was probably Wraysbury Mill (aka Culvett Mill), sited on the Colne Brook at the end of what is now Old Mill Place, off Coppermill Road. It has gone through a number of different incarnations, being used for the production of corn, silk and snuff but mostly paper or metal. It was a paper mill from at least 1605, turned to iron in 1772 and then copper under the ownership of Thomas Williams, the well-known copper magnate from Bisham and Horton. In 1844, Abbotson and Ladell took the mill back to paper production but, in the 20th century, it was turned into an industrial factory complex. The Bell Punch Co generated hydro-electricity there to make public transport ticket machines. The mill closed in 1971.

Wraysbury Railway Station was opened in 1861 and nearby Sunnymeads Station in 1927, five years after the surrounding bungalow estate had been built for local commuters. The southern portion of Wraysbury Reservoir, built in 1967-70, used to be the site of Wraysbury Common, although the parish boundary has moved and this is now part of Stanwell. The Wraysbury Lakes, formed by gravel extraction in more recent years, are called North and South Lake, Village and Silverwings Lake, with the small Scuba Lake between the two.

Printed Resources

This is a list of some of the major works consulted over many years and revisited more recently. Primary sources in the Berkshire Record Office and the National Archives are not listed. Various articles in the 'Reading Mercury,' 'Berkshire Chronicle,' 'Berkshire Archaeological Journal,' 'Berkshire Old and New' and 'Windlesora' and publications of Thames Valley Archaeological Services are not listed individually.

Astill, Grenville G (1978) Historic Towns in Berkshire: An Archaeological Appraisal. Reading: Berkshire Archaeological Committee

Ayling, Geoffrey M and Smith, Ian (2014) Admiral Arthur Forrest: Biography, Genealogy and Realated Lines of Descent. San Francisco: Blurb Inc

Babtie Group Ltd's Public Services Division (1994) Prehistoric Berkshire. Shinfield: Berkshire County Council

Babtie Group Ltd's Public Services Division (1995) Bastions of Berkshire: Medieval Castles. Shinfield: Berkshire County Council

Babtie Group Ltd's Public Services Division (1995) Roman Berkshire. Shinfield: Berkshire County Council

Babtie Group Ltd's Public Services Division (1996) Medieval Berkshire. Shinfield: Berkshire County Council

Baker, Jean (2003) Sandhurst: An Insight into the Larger Houses and Occupants. Sandhurst: Sandhurst Historical Society

Bannard, Henry E (c. 1985) A Short Sketch of the History of Littlewick. Littlewick Green: Henry E Bannard

Barham, Tony (1973) Witchcraft in the Thames Valley. Bourne End: Spurbooks Ltd

Barty-King, Hugh (2001) Warfield: A Thousand Years of a Berkshire Parish. Warfield: Warfield Parish Council

Bayley, Michael (1990). Personal Correspondence. Nash Ford Manuscript: M. Bayley

Baynes, Simon et al. (2000) The Winkfield Chronicles. Winkfield: Winkfield History Project Group Publishers

Beckinsale, RP (1972) Companion into Berkshire. Bourne End: Spurbooks Ltd

Berkshire Federation of Women's Institutes (1939) The Berkshire Book. Reading: Berkshire Federation of Women's Institutes

Betjeman, John and Piper, John (eds) (1949) Murray's Berkshire Architectural Guide. London: John Murray

Birney, Nan (1973) Bray Today and Yesterday. Maidenhead: Thames Valley Press

Bond, Maurice (1984) The Story of Windsor. Newbury: Local Heritage Books

Bonham, Valerie (1992) A Place in Life: The Clewer House of Mercy 1849-83. Windsor: Valerie Bonham

Bootle, Robin and Valerie (1990) The Story of Cookham. Cookham: R and V Bootle

Brain, John A (1904) Berkshire Ballads and Other Papers. Reading: Thomas Thorp

Brindle, Steven (ed.) (2018) Windsor Castle: A Thousand Years of a Royal Palace. Westminster: The Royal Collection

Brindle, Steven and Kerr, Brian (1997) Windsor Revealed: New Light on the History of the Castle. London: English Heritage

Brooks, EAS (1984) Maidenhead and its Name. Maidenhead: EAS Brooks

Burfitt, David (c. 1990) The Church of St Mary the Virgin, Hurley-on-Thames. Hurley: Hurley Parochial Church Council

Burrows, Montagu (1886) The Family of Brocas of Beaurepaire and Roche Court. London: Longman Green and Co

Caswall, Katherine (1921) Recollections of Binfield. Binfield: K. Caswall

Chambers, Jill (1999) Berkshire Machine Breakers: The Story of the 1830 Riots. Letchworth: Jill Chambers

Collins, Diane (2000) Easthampstead: Its Manor, Church and People. Bracknell: Juniper Publications

Collins, Diane (2019) Who owned South Hill Park? Bracknell: Diane Collins

Compton, Piers (1973). The Story of Bisham Abbey. Maidenhead: Thames Valley Press

Costin, Diana (1999) Grave Tales from Berkshire. Seaford: SB Publications

Cowley, Amanda, Cowley, Chris and Cleaver, Alan (1986) Strange Berkshire. Slough: The Strange Folklore Society

Dancy, Kitty (1987) History of Sandhurst. Sandhurst: K Dancy

Darracott, Ann (2014) An Account of the Personalities once represented in the Armorial Glass of the C14th St John the Baptist Church, Shottesbrooke. Maidenhead: Maidenhead Civic Society

Davenport, Hester (1995) Writers in Windsor. Old Windsor: Cell Mead Press

Davenport, Hester et al (2001) Windsor: A Thousand Years, A Living History. Windsor: Windsor Local History Publications Group

Davenport, Hester et al. (ed.) (2001) Windsor: A Thousand Years. Windsor: Windsor Local History Publications Group

Delaney, Peter (ed.) (1998) The Second Book of Wargrave. Wargrave: Wargrave local History Society

Dils, Joan and Yates, Margaret (eds) (2012) An Historical Atlas of Berkshire. Reading: The Berkshire Record Society

Ditchfield, Peter Hempson (1920) Byways in Berkshire and the Cotswolds. London: Robert Scott

Dumbleton, Michael (1978) Brickmaking: A local Industry. Bracknell: Bracknell and District Historical Society

Dunsbier, Matthew (1993) A Brief History of Binfield Place. Binfield: Matthew Dunsbier

Farndon, Doris, Mayne, Miranda, Millward, Joyce, Perkins, Angela, Shorland, Eileen and Stirling, Brends (eds) (1979) The Old Berkshire Village Book. Newbury: Countryside Books and Berkshire Federation of Women's Institutes

Farrar, Henry (1990) Windsor Town and Castle. Chichester: Phillimore and Co Ltd

Fenley, Pauline (1999) Sir John Kederminster's Library. Langley: Trustees of Sir John Kederminster's Library

Finn, Margot and Smith, Kate (2018) The East India Company at Home 1757-1857. London UCL Press

Fitzgerald, Della (2018) Hidden Bisham. Marlow: Marlow Museum

Ford, David Nash (2006) The Legends of Windsor Forest. Wokingham: Nash Ford Publishing

Ford, David Nash (2009) Berkshire in the Reign of Henry VIII. Wokingham: Nash Ford Publishing

Foreman, Stuart, Hardy, Alan and Mayes, Andrew (2001) The Excavation of Medieval and Post-Medieval Remains at Poyle House, Berkshire. Oxford: Oxford Archaeological Unit

Fraser, Maxwell (1973) The History of Slough. Slough: Slough Corporation

Gelling, Margaret (1982) The Place-Names of Berkshire Volumes 1-3. Birmingham: English Place Name Society

Gilson, Margaret (1995) Buildings of Old Windsor. Old Windsor: MF Gilson

Gray, Rosemary and Griffiths, Sue (eds.) (1986) The Book of Wargrave. Wargrave: Wargrave local History Society

Green, TK (1977) Iron Age Bracknell: Caesar's Camp. Bracknell: Bracknell and District Historical Society

Hadland, Tony (1992) Thames Valley Papists. Buckland: Tony Hadland

Harman, John (2004). The Caswalls and Victorian Binfield. Binfield: J. Harman

Harris, J and Stantan, GM (1971) A History of Winkfield. Winkfield: J Harris and GM Stantan

Harwood, T Eustace (1929) Windsor Old and New. London: T Eustace Harwood

Hedley, Olwen (1950) Round and About Windsor and District. Windsor: Oxley and Son (Windsor) Ltd

Hedley, Olwen (1967) Windsor Castle. London: Robert Hale Limited

Herbert, Stan (1987) The Charters Story. Sunninghill: De Beers Industrial Diamond Division

Hickson, Colin (1984) Bygone Bracknell. Chichester: Phillimore and Co Ltd

Hill, Mick (2016) Berkshire's Bareknuckle Battles 1777-1881 Peterborough: Fastprint Publishing

Hodder, FC (1937) A Short History of Sunningdale. London: Saint Catherine Press

Homes, Peter J (1992) St. Michael and all Angels, Sandhurst: History and Guide. Sandhurst: Sandhurst Parochial Church Council

Hudson, Helen (1989) Cumberland Lodge. Chichester: Phillimore and Co Ltd

Hughes, GM (1890) A History of Windsor Forest, Sunninghill and the Great Park. London: Ballantyne, Hanson and Co

Hunt, Violet G (c. 1980) A History of Fernhill Park. Bracknell: VG Hunt

Hunt, Violet G (1991) Martins Heron: A House and its Occupants. Bracknell: Bracknell and District Historical Society

Hunt, Violet G (1991) Lily Hill House: A Family History. Bracknell: Bracknell and District Historical Society

Hunter, Judith (2003) A Short History of Colnbrook. Colnbrook: Colnbrook with Poyle Parish Council

Ingram, Christine (1985) (ed) The New Berkshire Village Book. Newbury: Countryside Books and Berkshire Federation of Women's Institutes

Ingram, Christine (1990) (ed) Hidden Berkshire. Newbury: Countryside Books and Berkshire Federation of Women's Institutes

Ingram, Christine and Tony and Ridley, Pamela (eds) (1976) The History of Some Berkshire Inns and their Signs. Reading: Berkshire Federation of Women's Institutes

Jones, HA, Douglas-Sim, H and Burstall, Patricia (1990) The Story of All Saints' Parish Church, Bisham. Bisham: Bisham Parochial Church Council

Keen, Laurence and Scarff, Eileen (ed.) (2002) Windsor Medieval Archaeology, Art and Architecture of the Thames Valley. Leeds: British Archaeological association and Maney Publishing

Kennish, Janet (1999) Datchet Past. Chichester: Phillimore and Co Ltd

Kerry, Charles (1861) The History and Antiquities of the Hundred of Bray. London: Charles Kerry

Kidd-Hewitt, David (2004) Berkshire Tales of Mystery and Murder. Newbury: Countryside Books

Lack, William, Stuchfield, H Martin and Whittemore, Philip (1993) The Monumental Brasses of Berkshire. Piccadilly: Monumental Brass Society

Leach, Stephen (1985) The A'Bear Family of Wargrave. Wargrave: Wargrave Local History Society

Litson-Smith, Leslie (1999) The Cox Green Roman Villa. Cox Green: The Cox Green Local History Group

Long, Roger (1990) Murder in Old Berkshire. Buckingham: Barracuda Books Ltd

Long, Roger (2011) Haunted Berkshire. Stroud: The History Press McLoughlin, Ian (1992) Berkshire Murders. Newbury: Countryside Books

MacNaghten, Angus (1986) Haunted Berkshire. Newbury: Countryside Books

Marsdon, Jonathan and Winterbottom, Matthew (2008) Windsor Castle Official Souvenir Guide. London: Royal Collection Enterprises Ltd

Marson, Pamela and Mitchell, Brigette (2011) Windsor Guildhall: History and Tour. Windsor: Friends of the Windsor and Royal Borough Museum

McLoughlin, Ian (1992) Berkshire Murders. Newbury: Countryside Books

McLoughlin, Ian (1995) Ghosts of Berkshire. Newbury: Countryside Books

Millson, Cecilia (1977) Tales of Old Berkshire. Newbury: Countryside Books

Millson, Cecilia (1986) Old Berkshire Tales. Newbury: Countryside Books

Mitchell, Anne (1972) Ghosts along the Thames. Bourne End: Spurbooks Ltd

Morley, HT (1924) Monumental Brasses of Berkshire. Reading: Electric Press

Morris, John (ed) (1979) Domesday Book: Berkshire. Chichester: Phillimore and Co Ltd

Morris, Reg (1985) Distant Views from Sunninghill. Reading: Berkshire County Council

Morris, WJ and Crosland, Margaret (1970) Foliejon Park. Winkfield: Mining and Chemical Products Ltd

Morshead, Sir Owen (1957) Windsor Castle: An Illustrated History. London: Phaidon Press Limited

Munby, Julian; Barber, Richard and Brown, Richard (2007) Edward III's Round Table at Windsor. Woodbridge: The Boydell Press

Newton, Gordon (c. 1980) St. Michael and All Angels at Bray-on-Thames: The Story of a Famous Church. Bray: Bray Parochial Church Council

Nicolls, Jeff (1985) Our Mysterious Shire. Slough: Corinthian Publishers

Over, Luke (1969) Roman Influence in the Middle Thames Valley and Romano-British Sites in the Maidenhead area. Maidenhead: Maidenhead and District Archaeological and Historical Society

Over, Luke (1984) The Story of Maidenhead. Newbury: Local Heritage Books

Over, Luke (1986) Domesday Revisited: Windsor, Maidenhead and East Berkshire. Maidenhead: Thames Valley Booksellers

Over, Luke (1989) The Churches of Wealdham. White Waltham: White Waltham Parochial Church Council

Over, Luke (2009) Villages around Maidenhead. Stroud: The History Press

Over, Luke and Oppenheimer, Nicky (2001) Waltham Place and its Surrounding Parish. White Waltham: Nicky Oppenheimer

Over, Luke and Tyrrell, Chris (1993) The Royal Hundred of Bray. Bray: The Cliveden Press

Over, Luke and Tyrrell, Chris (1994) The Royal Hundred of Cookham. Bray: The Cliveden Press

Page, William; Ditchfield, Peter Hampson and Cope, John Hautenville (1906-23) The Victoria History of the County of Berkshire Volumes 1-3. London: St Catherine Press

Petry, Michael John (1972) Herne the Hunter: A Berkshire Legend. Reading: William Smith (Booksellers) Ltd

Phillips, Daphne (1983) The Great Road to Bath. Newbury: Countryside Books

Phillips, Daphne (1993) Berkshire: A County History. Newbury: Countryside Books

Pitt, Dennis (2014) Wraysbury, Ankerwycke and Magna Carta. Wraysbury: Magna Carta Committee of the Wraysbury Parish Council

Pooley, Lee (1977) Bracknell before the New Town. Bracknell: Allen Sharp

Pope, EB (1929) History of Wargrave. Hitchin: William Carling & Co

Railton, Margaret (2006) St. Lawrence's Church, Waltham St Lawrence: A Short History and Guide. Waltham St Lawrence: Margaret Railton

Railton, Margaret (2008) Ralph Newbery and the Bell Inn, Waltham St Lawrence. Waltham St Lawrence: Margaret Railton

Reid, Herbert J (1885) The History of Wargrave, Berks. Reading: W Smith

Roberts, Jane (1997) Royal Landscape: The Gardens and Parks of Windsor. London: Yale University Press

Roche, Jake H (2016) The Oakley Court, Windsor: The Story of Windsor's Most Iconic Hotel. Bray: Oakley Court

Rooney, Sheila and pat (1991). St Leonard's Hill Windsor. Windsor: Windsor Publications

Rosevear, Alan (2004) A Booklet on the Turnpike Roads around Reading. Kingston Bagpuize: Alan Rosevear

Rowse, AL (1974) Windsor Castle in the History of the Nation. London: Weidenfeld and Nicholson

St John-Hope, William Henry (1913) Windsor Castle: An Architectural History Vols 1 and 2. London: Country Life

Searle, CW (1937) The Origin and Development of Sunninghill and Ascot. Chertsey: TE Stevens and Son Ltd

Sears, RW (1930) History of Bracknell. Bracknell: RW Sears

Shorland, Eileen (1967) The Parish of Warfield and Easthampstead which includes the Old Bracknell. Warfield: Eileen Shorland

Stokes, Penelope (2005) Free Rein: Racing in Berkshire and Beyond. Hamstead Marshall: Penelope Stokes

Thorn, Peter (2000) Berkshire College of Agriculture: The History of Hall Place. Maidenhead: The Berkshire College of Agriculture

Tighe, Robert Richard and Davis, James Edward (1858) Annals of Windsor Volumes 1 and 2. London: Longman, Brown, Green, Longmans and Roberts

Timbrell, Ruth JC (1983) Chavey Up Down and Around. Winkfield: RJC Timbrell

Tucker, Joan (2012) Ferries of the Upper Thames. Stroud: Amberley Publishing

Tyack, Geoffrey; Bradley, Simon and Pevsner, Nicholas (2010) The Buildings of England: Berkshire. London: Yale University Press

Vansittart, Nicholas (1895) A Genealogical and Historical Account of the Family of Sittart now known as Vansittart. London: Mitchell and Hughes

Vincent, James Edmund (1931) Highways and Byways in Berkshire. London: MacMillan and Co Ltd

Watkinson, JA (c. 2000) What happened in Crowthorne before 1900. Wokingham: Maze Productions

Weightman, Christine (2000). Cheapside in the Forest of Windsor. Ascot: Cheapside Publications

Williams, Clive (2010) The Nabobs of Berkshire. Purley: Goosecroft Publications

Wilson, David Gordon (1977) The Making of the Middle Thames. Bourne End: Spurbooks Limited

Yarrow, Ian (1974) Berkshire. London: Robert Hale and Company

Young, Michael et al (2001) Public Houses of Sandhurst and Crowthorne. Sandhurst: Sandhurst Historical Society

Online Resources

Apart from my own Royal County of Berkshire History Website *www.berkshirehistory.com*, there are a number of good websites currently covering local history in East Berkshire:

Berkshire Turnpike Trusts
www.turnpikes.org.uk/Turnpikes in Berks.htm
Historical Cookham
vidbrook2.blogspot.com/2008/08
Historical Curiosities of Old Cippenham Village
ippenham.org
Oxford Dictionary of National Biography
www.oxforddnb.com
Postcards from Slough
www.postcards-from-slough.co.uk
Potted History of Sunninghill and Ascot
okthisandthat.org.uk/potted-history-of-sunninghill-and-ascot
Royal Windsor Website History Zone
www.thamesweb.co.uk/windsor/windsorhistory
Slough History Online
www.sloughhistoryonline.org.uk
Wexham Court Parish: The Origins of Slough – A Brief History
vexhamcourt.org.uk/TheOriginsofSlough.htm
The Workhouse: The Story of an Institution
www.workhouses.org.uk

Index